GRE®Prep

2020-2021

by

"The secret of getting ahead is getting started. The secret of getting started is breaking your complex overwhelming tasks into small manageable tasks, and then starting on the first one."

Mark Twain

Contents

Letter to Student   1

The Secrets, Unlocked!   3

Acknowledgements   4

Even More FREE Content!   5

About this Book   6

How to Use this Book   7

Preparing for Tests and Exams, Like a Professional   9

Mistakes Made on the GRE®   12

Some General (but Important) Information About the GRE®   13

General Tips and Advice   15

Verbal Reasoning   16

Quantitative Reasoning   22

Analytical Writing   37

Practice Test 1   56

    Section 1: Issue Topic   56

    Section 2: Argument Topic   58

    Section 3: Quantitative Reasoning   60

    Section 4: Verbal Reasoning   67

    Section 5: Quantitative Reasoning   74

    Section 6: Verbal Reasoning   81

    Answers   88

Practice Test 2   92

    Section 1: Issue Topic   92

    Section 2: Argument Topic   94

    Section 3: Quantitative Reasoning   96

    Section 4: Verbal Reasoning   103

    Section 5: Quantitative Reasoning   110

    Section 6: Verbal Reasoning   117

    Answers   124

Score Conversion   128

The Final Day and Night, Last Advice   135

Signing Off   137

Letter to Student

Dear Student,

Thanks for buying the GRE® prep 2020 2021 Study Guide.

This book was written for you, by experts in their fields. We spoke to many students and teachers to find exactly what they thought were missing in GRE® prep books. They told us that the test prep books are too bulky, too padded and too boring to read cover to cover. As a result, they felt that they were missing out on key hints and tips.

We asked them what they wanted and they said a simple guide written by someone who has actually sat the GRE®, by someone who has actually studied for the GRE® and by someone who actually aced it! So that's what we did.

We have produced a condensed book that you can read in its entirety. That you can get all the hints and tips that you need, and that you can trust that will improve your GRE® score and get you into the graduate school of your dreams.

You won't find long winded explanations and a text book style approach. You will find a useful study guide, hints, tips and strategies that real students have used on real GRE® papers and have scored really good scores with.

You will find two completely unique GRE® full length papers designed to prepare you to your absolute maximum. You will find examples and strategies to scoring on each test format. You will find extra hints and tips about performing to your very best.

Essentially, we have produced a book that was requested by you.

If you have any queries, further suggestions, or you feel that something is missing please do email info@innotion.org. We would love to hear from you, our test prep materials are designed with you in mind so please let us know if you would like to see something new!

Kind Regards

Innotion Academic Prep Ltd

The Secrets, Unlocked!

This book is not a text book. What this book is, is a breakdown of how to answer the questions, how to prepare and how to get the maximum score that you can do in your GRE®. It is the Secret Code to success in the world of the GRE®. We have unlocked the GRE® and made it accessible for all. Follow the instructions you are given on preparation, performance and review and you will get the score you need on your GRE®.

Acknowledgements

We would like thank publicly, the numerous professors, lecturers, students, teachers and tutors who have helped make this possible. When we spoke to others who struggled with the GRE® whom weren't as fortunate as to have access to the knowledge in this book, we knew we needed to write it. Without all of you contributors who either offered questions, reviews or just commentary, this book would not help the 1000s of students it has helped so far. Thank you.

Even More FREE Content!

This is a book forming part of a series of GRE® help books, tests and web content. Thank you for buying it and good luck in your GRE®. We have even more good news for you, we are working on 2 brand new tests and we will be delighted to send them to you as soon as they are ready at no cost! Simply send an email with your amazon order number at info@innotion.org, and we will do the rest.

About this Book

This book was written by Innotion Ltd for those students wanting to score 330 plus on their upcoming GRE® exam. It is designed to give you all the secrets, hints and tips to maximizing your scores and getting the candidate into the graduate school of their dreams!

The book has been written with painstaking effort and collaboration with teachers and students alike. We have spoken directly with students who have gone through the GRE® and scored amazing scores. We've gotten the exact hints and tips that they used to get into Ivy League Schools and now we are going to deliver that expertise to you!

It is a fast paced book, and we have kept it fluff free. You won't find long and drawn out explanations of high school concepts. What you will find is questions, with solutions and lots of strategies, hints, and tips for performing at your very best in an exam. This book is condensed and to the point, we have deliberately avoided lengthy explanations and unnecessary content.

Each section assumes some basic graduate level skills and knowledge, and then delves deeper into how to actually convert this graduate level schooling into an excellent score on the GRE®.

How to Use this Book

As we've said already, this book is a study guide, and not a text book. It is best read through from cover to cover once you have a basic knowledge of high school and college concepts in English and Math. When you are happy that your basic skills are up to speed, read the book. Pay close attention to the hints, the tips and the strategies. Make notes as you go. Jot down the key information in your study guide, use margins or even post-it's; a study skill in itself and it will help you to remember the hints we gave you. In the high stakes environment of the exam room it is all so easy to forget the little snippets of advice that ultimately make a big difference to your score.

Once you have read through the first part of the book with hints and tips, practiced the questions and feel like you are ready to go – take the first practice test.

This is a daunting moment, as you prepare for your test day. This should be done many weeks in advance, and (not the day before!). Do this in real exam conditions. Lock yourself in a room, remove any unnecessary technology and set up a timing system for the exam and stick to it; this part is often overlooked and yet is incredibly important, one of the major mistakes students make on the GRE® is to run out of time or worse to have excess time left over (therefore suggesting they may have rushed through questions earlier and tripped up!). This won't happen to you though; if you practice it correctly!

Once you've done the first practice test, take a break. Don't immediately mark it. This is another really useful hint: Students very often want to know exactly how they did in a practice exam but this is not the best use of your time, you're tired – exhausted even at this point and scoring your test is part of the learning process, as such take a rest, at least an hour but better if it's a day. Go away and do something fun, get some exercise, see some friends or play some sport. Then when you are fresh and academically alert you can score your test. When doing so write down the questions you get wrong, and crucially, why you got them wrong. Don't berate yourself for them, just note them down. The purpose of the first practice is exactly that: to practice! So, learn from it. Make sure the marking process is more than just scoring the exam but it is a learning process too!

When you've done that, go back and look at the practice questions you got wrong, work through them slowly, noticing what mistakes you made when did them first. (Go through them several times in different orders –it is useful if you don't immediately throw your first practice answers in the trash).

If then: you are happy that you have mastered the questions you got wrong, happy with those that you got correct and are ready to implement the new knowledge you have gained from the first test, go for the second.

As before you need to make sure you sit the test in the exam conditions. This should be about a week before the exam. Follow the same routine as earlier, do it in a separate room with a timer, take breaks when you should. Then take a rest and score it.

Hopefully by this stage in your preparation you will be scoring the sorts of scores that you want to be scoring in the final exam and will be happy. But if you're not, get some help on the questions you're getting wrong, there are many places you can look for help, but this book is certainly one of them!

If you've prepared correctly you will have nothing to worry about and this test result will be what you want. Take confidence from this: know that you have walked through the situation you will face at least two times now, and you have come out of it with your head held high and with a good score. That knowledge on the day of the exam will fill you with the confidence that you need to think calmly, coolly and to score what you have worked so hard for, and deserve!

Preparing for Tests and Exams,
Like a Professional

The GRE® is often the first step on the road towards a highly successful professional career.

So as the saying goes: "fake it till you make it!" If you want to have a professional career and you want that great job, a great degree and that great GRE® score... you must start acting professionally now. We don't mean wearing a suit all the time, we mean prepare for the GRE® like you would prepare for your dream job interview.

So, we spoke to teachers and graduates of the GRE®, and have collated the best and most useful hints, tips, and strategies for proper, professional exam preparation. Surprise – it is not best practice to cram and panic and do the exam after and all-nighter.

Many students will tell us (and you) " this is what works for me". Placing too much importance on the experiences and advice of others is not a winning strategy. Everyone is different, and everyone's experience of the GRE® is different. This being said, there are a few tried and tested strategies and behaviors which have the potential to boost every student's GRE® score. Even if those students do well (some do) they could all do better, probably much better if they followed some of the below advice for preparing for their exams.

The hints and tips below are the recipe for an aspirational, soon to be successful, GRE® applicant.

1. Strategies for when you are actually studying

- Keep on top of your work load, whatever you are studying, if you have a job, chores, tasks that you need to do, do not allow it to pile up. Make sure you set aside time each day, however brief, to focus on GRE® prep – a little goes a long way. Not only is this really good practice for a future busy life, it allows the time spent studying to be most effective with all your mind concentrated on your work, it doesn't pay to be distracted by an overwhelming amount of other things going on several short, sharp bursts of high concentration will yield tangible improvements.

- **Don't cram at the last second.** As we said earlier, this doesn't work. If you have bought this book, you have shown the first sign of being serious about improving in the GRE®. So, don't cram and don't plan on cramming. Do the hard yards now and they will pay off!

- **Practice tests.** Complete a Practice Exam (or both ideally!) Practice makes perfect. We have provided you with two GRE® past papers to get a feel for what it will be like on the day. Treat these papers like the real thing and push yourself to achieve your absolute best. But don't forget, this is one of the most important parts!

- **Distractions.** Study, and only study. Studies have shown that distractions during study periods significantly reduce focus, understanding and information retention. When you are preparing for the GRE®, try to rid yourself of all distractions. Set your cell to 'do not disturb', leave your laptop in another room, and get in some quality time with just you and this book.

- **Make a study group.** If you are part of a group of people all working towards a common goal this will help you focus and help you prepare effectively. It will give you a source of questions to answer. The important thing is not to get distracted when you meet. Create a plan for your meeting, how long you will spend on each area and exactly what you want to achieve. If, outside of this you enjoy their company then that's great, but during the pre-planned working hours is a great way to stay focused and keep making progress.

- **Reflect on your strategies.** As you progress through the act of preparing for your GRE® you are not only learning about the GRE® but also about your own self and your own study habits, reflect and see what is working and what isn't. Adjust these as you progress.

- **Pick an essay topic for yourself and draft a quick essay plan.** You can write on literally any topic – scanning the front page of the newspaper is a great place to start. Find an article presenting an issue and map out a plan of how you would explain two different sides of an argument might be and prepare draft essays for some. (You cannot do all of them, but the process of planning some will help you incredibly on the day).

2. Strategies to support your revision periods

- Routines

- **Plenty of rest.** Rest, rest and rest properly. One major influencer on your memory and subsequent performance is how much rest you get. You need to get at 8 hours sleep, during this time your mind will synthesize the information and you will be really well prepared.

- **Connecting with other students.** Get help. If you see something you don't understand, look it up in this book initially. If that doesn't do the trick then widen your search. Ask your fellow students, if possible, or if not, consult internet forums. If you have having particular difficulty with a concept, it's likely many people have had similar difficulties and have shared their experiences, strategies and solutions online. Get the help early and make sure that you understand it when you have done so. Don't suffer through it in silence!

- Also, maybe a point about spreading your revision time equally over the sections, with a little bit of weighting towards the section you find most difficult. If you have a quantitative background and are therefore more comfortable with the quantitative section, then the temptation is to spend more time on this section because it gives you a feeling of success. In reality, its best to focus on your weaknesses. Even if it makes revision a little more challenging and arduous: it will yield the best results in the end.

- **Link the content you are studying to your life or proposed career.** Linking information to personal experiences is a tried and tested way to improve memory and knowledge retention. Ever wondered how people can memorize an entire deck of cards – this is how! Personalization of information is the most powerful tool of memory experts. It is a really simple trick, that when used correctly can be incredibly effective.

3. Strategies for the test day

- **Have a good "game day" routine.** Practice it. Taking the time to prepare yourself properly for the day. Wake up early, change out of your pyjamas, eat a hearty breakfast and get yourself in the right mindset for the day ahead. A lot of excellent sports teams for example will train at a venue before playing in a fixture. They want as few new experiences on the test day as possible. This is the same for you.

- **Have a plan of attack.** With regard to each section of the test: how will the first 30 seconds look? What will do in the first two minutes? If you have a plan of attack, you will feel much more confident and these small margins are what dictate whether you get a good or exceptional score.

- **Check your answers**

- Read the instructions carefully, better yet; know the instructions in advance, and simply check them on the day.

- More detail later but, plan your essay questions!

- Process of elimination on the multiple choice questions is an absolute must. There is more detail on this later in this book, but remember to use it!

- **Use your time effectively and don't be afraid to skip ahead.** If something will take up more time than it is worth, skip it and answer the questions that you find easier to answer before returning and targeting the missed marks.

- **Focus on the question at hand.** One thing at a time. Focus entirely on the question you are trying to answer. Try not to fixate on questions you answered previously, or questions that might be asked later in the exam. Give you undivided attention to the question at hand: this will allow you to keep thinking clearly and avoid reaching cognitive overload. Not the next one on the one before, that one! It is completely ineffective to think about other questions when you are working on one, so focus on making the most of the time that you have!

- **Use extra time.** If you have some time left at the end: use it! Go back and check. Make sure you've answered everything, and that no questions are left blank. There's no negative marking on the GRE® so don't worry about guessing if you are really unsure of the answer.

- **Give yourself a reward if you've done well.** Praise yourself. Take a cup of coffee and sit outside, have some chocolate. The brain responds well to praise and rewards. So, if you deserve some: Have some!

Mistakes Made on the GRE®

People make mistakes, we know it. But a mistake is only a mistake if you make it twice, if you do it once: it is a lesson.

We've spoken to GRE® students, past and present and asked them for their biggest mistakes, the reason? So that you can learn the lesson, and not make their mistakes!

1. Being cheap with study materials. – Students have tried (and often failed) to pass the test without buying a book like this! The GRE® is a general test of your abilities, but there is more to it than just turning up: like anything good preparation is key! Trying to save money by skipping out on a test prep book is like trying to pass a driving test in a broken down car. Invest in yourself and you will see the benefits.

2. Saving all practice questions for the week of the exam. You should be practising regularly and often – even if it's just a few questions a day. Don't save all the questions for the week before. Many people save practice tests for the week in which they sit the test and then realize they don't know how to do them. Granted: you may not have half a day spare to do a full length paper every weekend, but do some questions, all the time.

3. Underestimating the difficulty of the quantitative section. Yes, it's high school math, yes you have the skills. But this is not a walk in the park. Particularly in the high pressure environment of test day. Practice it in depth and properly and you will be OK. But leave it out of your study plan and you will be in big trouble!

4. The Verbal section is not just knowing the Vocab. Yes, it's important that you be familiar with GRE® style vocabulary, (on their website) but, it is much more than that, on over half the questions, knowing the vocab alone won't help. This means that it is not always the right idea to spend ages learning all the words. Familiarize yourself with the vocab, of course. But do not try and remember every word that the GRE® exam uses.

5. Not sitting the exams under exam conditions. On the day, you will be stressed, of course you will! It's important. In order to be as prepared as possible you must practice the situation you will face. Do not make this mistake.

Some General (but Important) Information About the GRE®

The GRE® is an excellent test of your ability to succeed in the highly coveted MBA and other prestigious master's degree programs. Make no mistake, this is a sought after qualification held in high regard by the finest most prestigious graduate schools.

GRE® Structure

The GRE® is composed of three main sections: Quantitative Reasoning, Verbal Reasoning, and Analytical Writing. The first part of the GRE® is always analytical writing followed by verbal reasoning and quantitative reasoning. After analytical writing, verbal reasoning and quantitative reasoning can be presented in any order. The exam is expected to take approximately 3 hours and 45 minutes to complete.

Verbal Reasoning

The verbal test is scored between 130-170. Generally, the exam will consist of sections of 20 questions that have to be answered in 30 minutes. This set of questions can roughly be broken down into: 4 sentence equivalence, 6 text completion, and 10 reading comprehension questions.

In 2011 a raft of new questions was introduced to this section. These new questions shifted the emphasis of this section to an understanding and familiarity with vocabulary.

Quantitative Reasoning

These questions have been designed to test your high school level mathematics skills. The scoring is the same as the verbal reasoning, coming in between 130-170 with marks awarded in single-point increments. Again, this section is normally broken down into 20 questions. These are often broken down further as follows: 4 data interpretation questions, 8 quantitative comparisons, and 8 problem-solving questions.

Similarly to the verbal reasoning new questions were added to this portion of the test in 2011.

Issue Task

In this section, you are given a selected topic on which you must write an essay, in this book we will introduce you to the style of this essay questions and provide you with some invaluable examples of topics which may come up. In the issue essay, you will be presented with a point of view and asked to take a position on the issue. In essence, you will have to argue why your position is correct, giving a convincing account of your reasons and rationale. You have 30 minutes to write the issue essay.

Argument Task

For this test element you the test taker will be presented with a statement, you will then be required to evaluate this argument and write an article with your findings.

You will then be asked to report on the validity of the argument and asked to offer and apply reasoning which will improve both the quality and accuracy of the argument. It is important that you carry out this task from a purely logical point of view and not get embroiled in an emotional response.

Experimental Section

This section of the test can be either quantitative or verbal and will contain completely new questions. This section will not count towards your final score, but you will not be aware which section is the experimental section. It will appear identical to the scored sections of the test, for this reason, it is imperative that you answer all sections equally and do not attempt to guess which is the experimental section.

2011 Update

In 2011 the computer-based sections of the test were updated in quite a major way. The test no longer changes after each problem as it once did. It now only changes between the halves of each category. The difficulty of the second section of each category can vary depending on how well you performed in the first section. The algorithm has a vast pool of questions to pick from which each assigned a varying level of difficulty. If you do well in the first section and are given the harder questions in the following section you have the ability to earn a higher score on these more difficult questions. This difficulty scaling does not apply to the paper-based test.

General Tips and Advice

This section is intended to complement the advice given at the beginning of the book. These tips and general advice have been picked up after many years of experience with the GRE® exams.

Get off to a good start

The GRE® is designed as such that each question counts equally towards your overall grading. There will always be some questions that are well suited to your knowledge and abilities. Because each correct answer is weighted the same on the paper test it is very useful to answer the questions you feel most comfortable with first. You may find that you run out of time, it is a lot better to run out of time with a question remaining that you would have struggled to answer rather than one you feel you could have done well on.

Make a note and come back to it later

If you come across a particularly taxing question or even just one you feel may take a while to answer, then mark it and come back to it later. Use your time wisely and focus on questions you can answer with a high degree of accuracy. There will always be questions you struggle with. If you are spending too much time on a question, come back to it later on. This will mean you will not waste valuable time grappling with a tricky question and also, leaving the question and revisiting it later might give you a new perspective or allow you to look at the question with a fresh pair of eyes. Do not want to expend lots of time and energy on tough questions when there will be easier questions lurking deeper into the paper.

Multiple-choice questions

In some of the questions, you will be presented with multiple choice answers. One good trick here is to not try to answer perfectly the first time but rather to remove the incorrect answers on your first pass, returning to the question later with a smaller pool of possible answers. Sometimes you may not even know the correct answer but can work it out using a process of elimination. Even if you don't get rid of all of the possible incorrect answers each one you remove increases your chances of guessing correctly if you have to take a guess.

Use your spare paper

You are given 6 pieces of scratch paper to use for notes and workings and you can always ask for more. It is important to use this paper to lay out your thinking, getting it out of your head and down on a piece of paper can be crucial, particularly when returning to a question later in the test.

Forget what is done

When starting a new section of the paper it is important to forget about the previous sections. You may have struggled with the previous section but this next one will feature completely different questions which may suit you better; do not dwell on the questions you can no longer change.

Verbal Reasoning

This section of the GRE® is intended to measure your proficiency in analyzing and then evaluating written material. It is created to see how well you can take written information, digest, and understand it.

The reading comprehension questions are specifically designed to evaluate your ability to comprehend the forms of writing you will frequently encounter in graduate school.

For some of this section, you will be asked to read statements and passages and then asked to answer questions on the passages you have read. In other questions, you will be given an incomplete section of writing which you will need to interpret and then complete. The types of questions can be categorized as follows: Text Completion, Reading Comprehension, and Sentence Equivalence.

This can take the following forms:

- Knowing the meaning and significance of individual words.

- Understanding the meaning of individual sentences.

- Your ability to draw conclusions from written text.

- Summarizing long text down into short segments.

- Your ability to understand data which may be incomplete and then inferring the missing data.

- Extract meaning from context.

- Identify key points in an argument.

The length of each reading comprehension passage can vary. They normally max out at 8 paragraphs long although this is not a set in stone limit. The text can be about anything and often is an unusual subject matter.

General Advice for Reading Comprehension

The subject matter of the reading comprehension passages will be diverse and often complex, however you do not need any background knowledge on the subject as everything you need to answer will be included in the passage.

One area you can be often tested on is knowing the difference between opinions and facts. Make sure you are making a clear distinction between the two as you read through the passage, there will often be questions trying to gauge your understanding of the differences here.

It is essential to recognize when the writer's argument changes from one theory to another, they may do this often and you need to pick up on it.

Also, be aware of the author making two arguments that contradict each other, this again can happen, and if it does you need to be aware and take note. You can spot this from phrases like 'conversley, some argue that.'

Multiple Choice Questions

This section of the test will provide you with multiple answers to choose from. They, however, are not a standard multiple-choice format where only one of the possible answers is correct. There may be multiple correct answers and you will be expected to select all of them.

When answering these multiple-choice questions, it is important you take every answer on its individual merits. Two answers may be very similarly written, but just because one is correct it does not always follow that a similar answer will also be correct. Do not try to rush through the answers here, take your time, and judge the merit of each answer individually. The test writers often like to throw in the odd curveball with partially correct answers, we must stress a partially correct answer is an incorrect answer. You have to be aware and not get caught out by these partially correct answers.

This multiple-choice section is really tricky, for this reason, it is imperative that you take your time here. The test writers like to get particularly deceptive here so keep an eye out for this. Just read and then re-read all of these questions and answers, a quick skim read will often lead to disaster.

Pick the Correct Sentence

This is a twist on the multiple-choice answer format. You will be given a description and then have to choose the sentence that best summerises with that description. As with the above multiple-choice section, slowing down and taking the time to deliberately and purposefully read through the statement and possible answers will bear fruit. It is essential not to rush these sections, you could quickly rush through and think you have aced this section only to find you got caught out by some nasty tricks!

Text Completion

This section of the test will test your ability to read, digest, and fully understand written text. You will be tasked with reading an incomplete passage and then filling in the blanks. There will often be answers that sound almost identical but have completely different meanings and could completely change the purpose of the text. In questions such as this, paying particular attention to the context (the sentences that come before and after the sentence with missing words) can be extremely helpful.

Sentence Equivalence

This portion of the test is intended to test your ability to understand a passage and then correctly select an answer to complete the passage. The sentence equivalence section expands on text completion by asking you to match meanings and writing styles. You will have to understand the prose of the text, fully comprehending how the individual author of the prose writes so that you can correctly fill in the blanks.

The questions are structured in the following way: an incomplete sentence with one blank to be filled and then six possible answers to fill in the blank. For each question you will have to provide two correct answers, you will receive zero marks for only selecting one potential answer. You must select two words from the list.

One pitfall many test-takers fall into in this section is trying to rush it, they will quickly search the possible answers for two answers that mean the same thing, thinking that must mean they are the correct answer. This is not always the case, the answers may mean the same thing but one may not match the structure and writing of the text, making it an incorrect answer. The key is to ensure that when your selected words are inserted into the sentence, the meaning of the passage does not change.

When you are reading through the given paragraph, always be thinking about what the sentence means, what the writer is trying to convey. You may find one answer that fits perfectly but then struggle to find a second that doesn't mean the same things as your first answer. If one word fits perfectly then it will be correct, you then need to look for a second answer that also fits. It will not necessarily have an obviously better choice, but rather, the overall meaning of the passage will be similar.

When you have completed the answers read through the full sentence individually with your answer plugged in. This is a great way to double-check your answer. Check that the sentence flows correctly, that the grammar is correct and that the outcome of each sentence is consistent.

GRE® Verbal Reasoning Examples

Text Completion

1. With profits dwindling, the company should immediately suspend all unnecessary expenditure and _____ activities in order to save money.

   A. untoward

   B. nugatory

   C. voluble

   D. prosaic

   E. quotidian

Correct answer: B

2. He found that the locals relied on superstition and (i) _____ to make town decisions, which often resulted in (ii) _____ outcomes.

Blank (i)	Blank (ii)
indomitability	infelicitous
sophistry	auxiliary
immutability	tractable

Correct answers: (i) sophistry, (ii) infelicitous

3. His curiosity for chemistry, and his (i) _____, led him to attempt to synthesis TNT in his home kitchen. When the police heard about these activities, they were simply (ii) _____: they informed the budding chemistry that attempting to synthesis TNT as home was (iii) _____ to domestic terrorism.

Blank (i)	Blank (ii)	Blank (iii)
incautiousness	embittered	peripatetic
lassitude	aghast	coeval
repugnance	heinous	tantamount

Correct answers: (i) incautiousness, (ii) aghast, (iii) tantamount

Sentence Equivalence

1. The Mennonites are a group of ultraconservative Christians who _____ technology and the modern world in favor of a simpler and more traditional life.

   A. chastise

   B. imbue

   C. eschew

   D. assuage

   E. forswear

   F. vitiate

Correct answers: C and E

2. Emperor Qin Shi Huang believed that consuming mercury was the secret to immortality. Historical documents suggest that this practice, over time, caused Emperor Huang to grow more erratic and _____.

   A. insatiable

   B. mercurial

   C. malevolent

   D. indomitable

   E. capricious

   F. facetious

Correct answers: B and E

Reading Comprehension

Alexander Pope was born on the brink of the Enlightenment period, when science shadowed over the past efforts of religion and the darker ages. As a catholic in a very anti-Catholic regime, Pope held the perspective of an outsider, looking into the world that he was not wholly accepted within. This was a time when England was enlarging its borders beyond the country of its own inhabitation; when science began to provide reason for the ways of the world, allowing new theories and revolutions to begin. In his Essay on Man, Pope hopes to emphasis Godly beliefs in order to tie back the world of reason to that of religion. Embodying his poem to the theory of the clockwork universe, Pope argues that everything that is in existence has a place in a much bigger establishment, declaring that 'Whatever Is, is Right'. Indeed, through the magnificent sentence structure and detailed imagery, Pope's ideology is exemplified in this text, allowing his argument for the Enlightenment period to resonate throughout the text, making it one of his most appreciated works.

1. The primary purpose of the passage is to:

    A. To explain, in detail, the poetic technique Alexander Pope utilised in his work.

    B. To explain one of the aims Alexander Pope hoped to achieve with his poetry.

    C. To document key moments in the Enlightenment period.

    D. To distance Alexander Pope's legacy from that of the Enlightenment period.

    E. To understand one of Alexander Pope's poems as a reflection of its context.

Correct answer: B

2. It is clear from the passage that the author regards Pope's poetry as:

    A. Trivial

    B. Reductive

    C. Masterful

    D. Superficial

    E. Enigmatic

Correct answer: C

3. According to the passage, Pope sort to:

    A. Champion science over religion.

    B. Champion religion over science.

    C. Unify science and religion so they can coexist.

    D. Promote catholic ideologies over all else.

    E. Voice his disdain for rising anti-Catholic sentiments in the country.

Correct answer: C

4. What is the primary purpose of the sentence highlighted above?

    A. To provide historical context to Pope's work.

    B. To rationalise Pope's religious perspective.

    C. To dismantle a common misconception regarding Pope's work.

    D. To confirm a common interpretation of Pope's work.

    E. To establish Pope as the seminal poet of his time.

Correct answer: A

5. In the context in which it is seen above, what does the word 'resonate' most nearly mean?

    A. Move erratically.

    B. Observed superficially.

    C. Vibrate repetitively.

    D. Present throughout.

    E. Completely absent.

Correct answer: D

Quantitative Reasoning

Many people like to say that the math included in this section of the test is fairly basic, and that is true, a lot of this you may have covered in high school. But, and this is a key point many people overlook, you may well have forgotten a lot of it. Some of these math skills are rarely used outside of school and as such we soon forget about them.

GRE® Geometry

In this portion of the test, your geometry skills will be put to the test. Your ability to solve mathematical problems using geometrical knowledge will be tested. One facet of this section that can be often overlooked by other prep books is that there is also quite a focus on problem-solving. Breaking the question down into small easily solvable chunks can often go a long way to helping you find the correct solution.

GRE® Problem Solving

This is the more obvious problem-solving section of the test, while it may be useful in the geometry portion to have good problem-solving skills, here in the quantitative section it is imperative. Within the problem-solving section of the quantitative questions, you will be faced with multiple-choice questions that can have many possible answers listed. As well as the multiple-choice there will also standard answer questions where you will be asked to provide your own numerical solution. There will be a small box in which to write your answer.

Remember, the test setters are often out to trick you on this quantitative question section. The questions may seem easy and you may think you are flying through the answers but just stop and take the time to double-check the questions and make sure you haven't fallen into any of the traps set by the test writer. Often when you have practiced these questions a few times the traps will become more obvious and you will be able to see when the test writer is trying to trick you.

Like a lot of math papers, it can be helpful on some questions to estimate the answer first before diving deeper. For a very basic example 258 x 33 can become 250 x 30 and you then know the ballpark that your figure should be falling into. This is a great way of quickly sanity checking your answers too. You won't be allowed a calculator in the exam, so tricks like this can save you a lot of time and hassle.

When preparing for this section of the test many students may try and cram and study as many different math problems as possible. This is not always the best route to success: it can often be overwhelming, and sometimes counterproductive. Sometimes practicing reading the questions correctly, slowing down, and methodically answering can provide a much better improvement to your score than simply cramming.

When practicing, always try and gradually ramp up the difficulty of your questions, this is the only way to score big on this test. You won't become an expert on this section quickly; it takes practice, but not just in math also in written comprehension and problem-solving.

GRE® Quantitative Reasoning Examples

1. $2a - 4b = 24$
   $5a + 2b = 30$

	Quantity A	Quantity B
	a	b

A. Quantity A is greater

B. Quantity B is greater

C. The two quantities are equal

D. The relationship cannot be determined from the information given

Correct answer: A

I. $2a - 4b = 24$

II. $5a + 2b = 30$

To find the value of a and b, the substitution method can be used to solve equations.

Thus, in I.:

$2a - 4b = 24$

$2a = 24 + 4b$

Then:

III. $a = \dfrac{24 + 4b}{2}$

Now, replace in II. the value of a. Then,

$5a + 2b = 30$

$5 \dfrac{24 + 4b}{2} + 2b = 30$

Multiplys both sides of the equation by 2 to eliminate the coefficient $\dfrac{1}{2}$

$5(24 + 4b) + 4b = 60$. Then,

$120 + 20b + 4b = 60$

$20b + 4b = 60 - 120$

$24b = -60$

$b = \dfrac{-60}{24}$

$b = -2.5$

Replacing the value of b in equation III.:

$$a = \frac{24 + 4 \times -2.5}{2} = \frac{24 - 10}{2} = \frac{14}{2} = 7$$

Then, a = 7 and b = -2.5.

2.

	Quantity A	Quantity B
	$(x + 9)^2$	$x^2 + 7$

A. Quantity A is greater

B. Quantity B is greater

C. The two quantities are equal

D. The relationship cannot be determined from the information given

Correct answer: D

Quantity A = $(x + 9)^2 = x^2 + 18x + 81$

Quantity B = $x^2 + 7$

A - B = $x^2 + 18x + 81 - x^2 - 7$

A - B = $18x + 74$.

Depending on the value of x, this difference can be negative or positive.

3. A team flag features black, blue and pink circles. A fifth of the circles are black. Half of the remaining circles are blue.

	Quantity A	Quantity B
	The number of pink circles.	The number of blue circles minus the number of black circles.

A. Quantity A is greater

B. Quantity B is greater

C. The two quantities are equal

D. The relationship cannot be determined from the information given

Correct answer: A

Black circles = $\frac{1}{5}$ of 100% = 20% of circles.

Total remaining circles = 100% - 20% = 80%

Blue circles = $\frac{1}{2}$ of 80% = 40% of circles.

Pink circles (quantity A) = Total remaining circles = 80% - 40% = 40%.

And quantity B is = 40% - 20% = 20% of circles.

4. y = (21)(15)(33)

Quantity A	Quantity B
the units digit	4

A. Quantity A is greater

B. Quantity B is greater

C. The two quantities are equal

D. The relationship cannot be determined from the information given

Correct answer: A

y = 21 x 15 x 33 = 10395.

The digit unit is 5, and 5 is greater than 4.

5. Every week, Julia buys seven times more cookies than Elisa and eats them all. Dora buys eight times more cookies than Elisa each week, but always gives three to her friends and eats the rest.

Quantity A	Quantity B
The number of cookies Julia eats each week.	The number of cookies Dora eats each week.

A. Quantity A is greater

B. Quantity B is greater

C. The two quantities are equal

D. The relationship cannot be determined from the information given

Correct answer: D

The list that expresses the number of cookies purchased by each one is: *(Note: J = Julia; E = Elisa; D = Dora).*

J = 7E

D = 8E - 3

Equalizing the two quantities:

7E = 8E - 3

7E - 8E = -3

E = 3

If Elisa buys < 3 cookies, then Julia eats more. However, if Elisa buys > 3 cookies, then Dora eats more.

6. Two right angled triangles are shown.

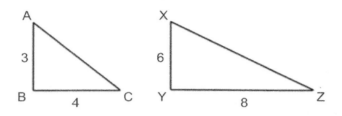

Note: Figure not drawn on the scale

Quantity A	Quantity B
3 x AC	XZ

A. Quantity A is greater

B. Quantity B is greater

C. The two quantities are equal

D. The relationship cannot be determined from the information given

Correct answer: A

Using the Pythagorean theorem:

$AC^2 = 3^2 + 4^2$

$AC^2 = 9 + 16$

$AC^2 = 25$

AC = 5

$XZ^2 = 6^2 + 8^2$

$XZ^2 = 36 + 64$

$XZ^2 = 100$

XZ = 10.

3AC = 3 x 5 = 15.

Thus, quantity A is greater.

7. A cylinder has a height of 5 cm and a radius of 3 cm, as shown.

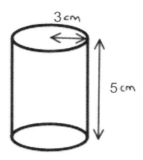

3cm

5 cm

Quantity A	Quantity B
The volume of the cylinder.	The volume of a sphere with radius 3 cm.

A. Quantity A is greater

B. Quantity B is greater

C. The two quantities are equal

D. The relationship cannot be determined from the information given

Correct answer: A

The volume of the **cylinder** is = r²hπ = 3² x 5 x π = 9 x 5 x π = 45π

The volume of the **sphere** is = $\dfrac{4r^3\pi}{3}$ = $\dfrac{4 \times 3^3 \times \pi}{3}$ = $\dfrac{4 \times 27 \times \pi}{3}$ = 36π

Thus, the volume of the cylinder is greater than the volume of the sphere.

8. ABDE is a square. C is exactly at the midpoint of line BD. Given that the length of AC is 3√5, find the length of one side of the square.

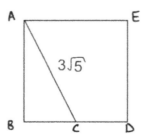

A   E

3√5

B   C   D

A. 4

B. 5

C. 6

D. 7

E. 8

Correct answer: C

Since a square has all sides equal and the side BC is half a side of the square, then BC can be written as $\dfrac{AB}{2}$.

Applying the Pythagorean theorem to this triangle we have:

$$AB^2 + \left(\frac{AB}{2}\right)^2 = (3\sqrt{5})^2$$

$$AB^2 + \frac{(AB)^2}{4} = 9 \times 5$$

Multiply both sides of the equation by 4. Then,

$$4AB^2 + AB^2 = 180$$

$$5AB^2 = 180$$

$$AB^2 = \frac{180}{5}$$

$$AB^2 = 36$$

$$AB = 6$$

9. Find the point at which the lines y = x - 4 and y = -2x + 2 intersect.

   A. (3,0)

   B. (-2,2)

   C. (2,4)

   D. (2,-2)

   E. (0,4)

Correct answer: D

To find the x coordinate that occurs at the intersection, it is necessary to equal the functions: Then,

x - 4 = -2x + 2

x + 2x = 4 + 2

3x = 6

$x = \dfrac{6}{3} = 2$

To find the value of y that this intersection occurs it is necessary to replace the value of x in one of the equations.

y (x) = x - 4. Then,

y (2) = 2 - 4 = -2

So, the point coordinates are (2, -2)

10. $2.6 \times 10^5 + 2.5 \times 10^5 + 12 \times 10^4$

Which of the following values is equal to the expression above?

    A. 6.3×10^5

    B. 63×10^5

    C. 63×10^3

    D. 63×10^4

    E. 6.3×10^4

Correct answers: A and D

To perform the addition of numbers in scientific digits it is necessary that they are all on the same basis, so it is necessary to transform the 12×10^4 in basis of 10^5. To do this, just move one decimal place of the number from right to left. Like this,

$12 \times 10^4 = 1.2 \times 10^5$

With all the numbers on the same base, you can add them all together and keep the base.

$2.6 + 2.5 + 1.2 = 6.3 \times 10^5$ which can also be represented by 63×10^4.

11. The owner of a large coffee shop works out that with a team of 6 barristas, his shop can make 30 coffees in 15 minutes. If he sacks two of his barristas, how long will it take the shop to make 45 coffees?

    A. 22 minutes

    B. 30 minutes

    C. 34 minutes

    D. 40 minutes

    E. 48 minutes

Correct answer: C

$\dfrac{30}{15} = 2$ coffes per minute with 6 barritas

INNOTI N
ACADEMIC PREP

$\dfrac{2}{6}$ = 0.33 coffes per minute per barrista

So now with 4 barristas we have 0.33 x 4 = 1.33 coffees per minute.

Which is $\dfrac{45}{1.33}$ = 33.8 = 34 minutes for 45 coffees.

12. Use the axes to calculate the area of the shape ABCDE.

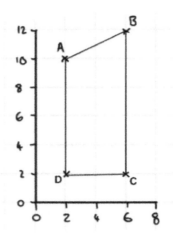

A. 24

B. 26

C. 30

D. 36

E. 42

Correct answer: D

The area above can be divided into two geometric figures: a rectangle and a triangle.

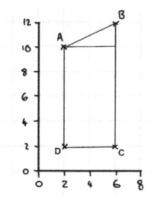

The area of the **rectangle** is given by: height x width = 8 x 4 = 32 units

The area of the **triangle** is given by: $\dfrac{\text{height x width}}{2} = \dfrac{2 \times 4}{2} = 4$ units.

The area of the figure is the area of the rectangle + the area of the triangle = 32 + 4 = 36 units.

13. What fraction of the circle shown is shaded yellow?

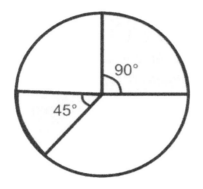

A. $\dfrac{1}{3}$

B. $\dfrac{1}{8}$

C. $\dfrac{2}{10}$

D. $\dfrac{3}{8}$

E. $\dfrac{7}{24}$

Correct answer: D

$90° = \dfrac{1}{4}$ of 360°

$45° = \dfrac{1}{8}$ of 360°

$90° + 45° = \dfrac{1}{4} + \dfrac{1}{8} = \dfrac{12}{32} = \dfrac{3}{8}$

14. Six friends want to play battleships. Each game of battle ships requires two players. How many games have to be played to ensure that every player plays every other player?

A. 8

B. 15

C. 22

D. 25

E. 28

Correct answer: B

Player 1 can play a game vs 5 opponents (Players 2, 3, 4, 5, 6) (5 Possible fixtures)

Player 2 can play a game vs 5 opponents (Players 1, 3, 4, 5, 6) but, 1vs2 is including in player 1's match list (4 Possible fixtures). Here: player 1's fixture list contains 1vs2 so you do not include it in player 2's fixture list. This idea of permutations and combinations continues below.

Player 3 can play a game vs 5 opponents (Players 1, 2, 4, 5, 6) but, 1 vs 3 and 2 vs 3 is including in player 2 and player 3's match list (3 Possible new fixtures)

Player 4 can play a game vs 5 opponents (Players 1, 2, 3, 5, 6) but, 1 vs 4, 2 vs 4 and 3 vs 4 is including in player 2, player 4 and player 4's match list (2 Possible new fixtures)

Player 5 can play a game vs 5 opponents (Players 1, 2, 3, 4, 6) but, 1 vs 5, 2 vs 5, 3 vs 5, 4 vs 5 are included in player 1, 2, 3 and player 4's match list (1 Possible new fixtures)

Player 6 can play a game vs 5 opponents (Players 1, 2, 3, 4, 5) but all these fixture's have already been accounted for in the other match lists (0 Possible new fixtures)

So, the total number of matches is 5 + 4 + 3 + 2 + 1 = 15.

15. If a, b and c sum to 15, 2b - a = 3 and 2c + b = 6, what is the value of ac?

   A. 0

   B. 2

   C. 15

   D. 25

   E. 27

Correct answer: A

I. $a + b + c = 15$

II. $2b - a = 3$

III. $2c + b = 6$

I. $b = 15 - c - a$

Into II. $2(15 - c - a) - a = 3$

IV. $2c + 3a = 27$

(IV. - III.) = 3a - b = 21

V. b = 3a - 21

Into II. 2(3a - 21) - a = 3

6a - 42 - a = 3

5a = 45

a = 9

Into IV. 2c + 27 = 27

c = 0

ac = 0

16. Michael takes 4 hours to paint a room. When Jim helps him, it only takes 90 minutes to paint the room. How long would it take Jim to paint the room on his own?

    A. 144 minutes

    B. 152 minutes

    C. 160 minutes

    D. 180 minutes

    E. 204 minutes

Correct answer: A

$$\frac{1}{t_1} + \frac{1}{t_2} = \frac{1}{t_0}$$

$$\frac{1}{4} + \frac{1}{t_2} = \frac{1}{1.5}$$

$$\frac{1}{t_2} = \frac{1}{1.5} - \frac{1}{4} = \frac{5}{12}$$

$$t_2 = \frac{12}{5} \text{ hours} = 144 \text{ minutes.}$$

17. If x is a positive integer, which expression below gives the number of integers that are greater than 2x -1 and smaller than 4x + 2?

    A. 2x + 1

    B. x + 2

C. x - 1

D. x - 2

E. 2x + 2

Correct answer: E

Choose 4 different numbers for x and substitute in your equations. In the bottom row of the table are the number of positive integers between the two numbers that are directly above them.

	x = 0	x = 1	x = 2	x = 3
2x - 1	-1	1	3	5
4x + 2	2	6	10	14
Number of positive integers	2	4	6	8

So,

I. When x = 0, there are 2 integers.

II. When x = 1, there are 4 integers.

III. When x = 2, there are 6 integers etc.

Consider y = numbers of integers. The expression that determines the number of integers is like: y = ax + b.

Using I., we get:

y = ax + b =

2 = a.0 + b =

2 = b

Then, the expression is like:

y = ax + 2

For found the value of a, using II.

4 = a.1 + 2

4 = a + 2

2 = a

So, the expression is: y = 2a + 2

The graph shows the results of a random sample of 7 students were asked to provide their weekly earnings and weekly expenditure. And refers to questions 18-20:

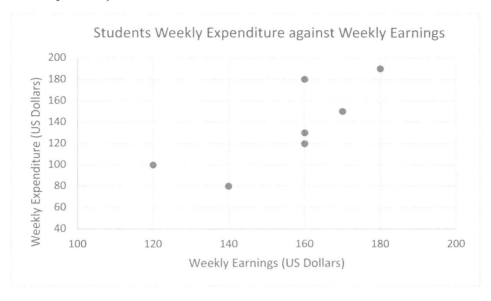

18. How many students spent less than they earned each week?

    A. 1

    B. 2

    C. 3

    D. 4

    E. 5

Correct answer: E

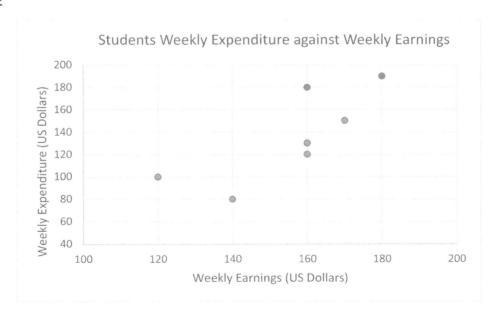

This question is to read the graph, for easy viewing, in the chart above, students whose earnings are greater than expenses are in green while students who occur the opposite are in red.

19. How many students spent the same of their earnings each week?

    A. 0

    B. 1

    C. 2

    D. 3

    E. 4

Correct answer: A

Using the graph in the previous question, it is clear that no student spends the same as he earns.

20. If every student in the sample received a 20% pay rise, what would the new range of weekly earnings be among the sample?

    A. 54

    B. 58

    C. 66

    D. 69

    E. 72

Correct answer: E

You need to take the highest earning person, and add 20%.

180 + 20% of 180 = 180 + 36 = 216

And then the lowest earning person and do the same:

120 + 20% of 120 = 120 + 24 = 144

Then to find the range is the 216 - 144 = 72

Analytical Writing

This section is where you can really score strongly and make yourself really stand out. Mastering the analytical writing section will take time and patience but it is possible, even a perfect score here is not out of the realm of possibility.

This section of the test contains two essay sections where you are given 30 minutes to complete each essay. It is important to note that this section of the test is just there to evaluate your writing ability. Your reasoning or argument is not relevant like in the other sections, as long as your argument is based in reality it does not matter, the only intention of these essays is to judge your writing ability.

While it is commonly accepted that a good score here is not as valuable as getting a good score on the other sections it is still really important. If you score really poorly here it will still stand out and could lead to doubt in the admissions officers' mind. In contrast to this, an excellent score here will be the icing on the cake and could be the thing that tips your admission process over the edge.

On analytical writing, you can score between 0 and 6.0 with 6 being a perfect score. Scores are given in 0.5 increments. The criteria an essay must meet to receive a perfect 6.0 is as follows:

Outstanding: a well-articulated attempt of successful writing and the ability to specifically define and examine the main features of the argument with profound insight. Develops cogent concepts, systematically organizes them, and integrates them without abrupt transformations. Strongly respects arguments' key points. Demonstrates superior English language knowledge, including pronunciation, sentence formation, spelling, grammar, and variation used in standard written English. No defects in the article.

Your essay will be read and assessed by two markers, they will read it independently and then give you a grade. The scoring is based on a set of pre-defined criteria. These criteria are things such as the effectiveness of your critical thinking as well as your writing ability. These two separate scores will then be combined to produce your final analytical writing score. If the two scores are given are more than one full point apart from a third, highly experienced, the grader is then called in to look at the differences and give a final overall score.

While the full scoring range falls between 0-6 almost all (around 90%) of scores fall within the range 2-5. This is why we talked earlier about how a perfect score here can set you apart from the majority of test-takers.

There are several main scoring areas taken account when grading, they are as follows:

Structure, clarity, vocabulary, sentence mixing, grammar, and logic.

1. Structure

The structure is an integral part of your essay, its formatting, readability & arrangement are integral to creating an essay that can be easily understood and digested. If there is no structure to your essay then your argument will not come across at all before writing, clearly define the key points you want to make and write roughly a

paragraph on each point. Start with your most compelling argument to show the reader that you really know what you're talking about.

2. Clarity

Clarity is one of the most critical and basic of all aspects on which the graders judge the essays. The grader will need to understand what you're saying, having read the essay once, and most likely, very quickly. It makes their job harder, and they will realize that if your argument can be understood with just one reading, the essay is a good essay. As we said earlier the grader does not spend long on the paper, so they really don't want to read it twice, as such, make simple ways to achieve this: don't use too many long and convoluted sentences. Make sure the first sentence of each paragraph clearly states the main point of the paragraph.

3. Vocabulary

Many previous test takers hold the belief that you will be rewarded for showing a strong vocabulary on the GRE®. So, demonstrating a deep vocabulary can be a massive advantage to you and lead to improved scores. A word of caution here though, do not use complicated vocabulary for the sake of it. If you can use logic, correct syntax, and intelligently justify your argument alongside displaying a good vocabulary you will be setting yourself up for a good score.

4. Sentence Mixing

While writing multiple paragraphs on the same subject, you should preferably avoid writing similar sentences. Consecutive sentences of the same structure and duration can sound monotonous and bland, and most importantly they are clearly boring for the reader. Instead of repetitive and dull sentences, use sentence structure skilfully. You don't have to rearrange the words, or change the voice from passive to active, or vice-versa. By flipping between short and long sentences, you can keep changing sentence structures, flow, and rhythm.

5. Grammar

While the official line is that you may have small errors in the essay, it doesn't mean you should overlook mistakes. While mistakes or defects do not interfere with general sense and accuracy, you will realize that when you make the first mistake on the document, the grader will note it and be more aware when reading the remainder of the text. Then any more mistakes you make are even more apparent.

6. Logic

Logic is crucial in assessing the essay's overall argument and quality. Find as much evidence as you can to back up what you say in your essay. One of the best features of a convincing article is the potential to persuade the listener by good logical thinking, clearly supported by relevant examples. Anyone who reads your answers should be completely persuaded by your point of view.

Essay Length

Whoever is grading your essay will be well aware that you only had 30 minutes to write it, they are not expecting War and Peace.

Quality over quantity matters here, a shorter but well-written piece will always outperform a longer, poor quality piece.

My advice is to write around 500-600 words. Studies demonstrate that this is an optimal amount of words for scoring. After 600, your essay appears rushed and mistakes creep in. Hence, we suggest 500-600 is a good amount of words to target.

Essay Subject

If you are dedicated enough, every single possible essay subject is listed on the official ETS website. However, there are around 200 of them! To try and write a practice essay on each of these subjects is just not practical and the time spent if you were to do that would detract from your performance on other sections of the test.

The subjects can be broken down into the following groups, so writing a practice essay on each of the following groups is a much better way to prepare for the test.

- Government

- Education

- Arts

- Politics

- Economics

- Sciences and Technology

GRE® Issue Essay Example

Below is an example issue essay with a response, this is a high scoring essay and is included to give you an idea of what a 6 essay looks like.

The essay is intended as a benchmark response — one that would earn a top score of 6. But it is by no means "the" correct response to the prompt. Other top-scoring essays might be organized differently, or make different points.

Colleges should require students to engage in public-service activities in order to assure that each student receives a balanced, well-rounded education.

An example answer to this is below:

Education is not just imparting academic knowledge amongst students. It is the development of all around personality of a student in order to make him eligible to adjust and succeed in the society. That is why along with

cognitive development, education should seek physical, cultural, moral and social development of the child. I agree with the statement that engaging students in public-service activities helps in their all-around development. I would like to add that this should be an extension to curriculum followed in schools for children's social development.

Moreover, along with engaging students in public-service activities, it is important to inculcate values like helpfulness, social responsibility and respect towards every work, even if it is small, so that they do not view any task as a menial job, and have the willingness to continue doing it in their later lives. Each individual is a member of the society. Therefore, it is important that students are educated about their role in the society. Every citizen of the society has a social responsibility. They need to realize their responsibility at the right time so that they perform their duties well. College is the pinnacle of student's education. It is here that they are finally prepared to face the world and be at their own. Hence, the curriculum of colleges should not only include the academic part, but must also concentrate on social education.

If the students are made to do works like cleaning a public park, extending help to patients like donating blood and helping poor to get food, medicines etc., it will develop a feeling of compassion amongst them for the needy and also make them realize their role as a responsible citizen.

It is often seen that the young misuse public utilities like water. Many times public taps are kept running and leaking. No one makes an effort to close these taps and save water. It is only when the students are made to do public services that they realize the importance of such things.

Therefore, if colleges step-in and encourage the students to avoid wasting water, and provide clean drinking water to the needy, it will help in building up good values and guidelines for them. This will encourage them to follow these guidelines throughout their lives. As I have mentioned earlier, it is not only the colleges that should keep in mind the all-around development of a student, but the schools should also ensure that they form the basis for the same.

Therefore, the curriculum in a school should also include social education where students should be taught the benefits of maintaining good social behaviour. It is only when our educational institutions help in inculcating such habits that we can have a healthy society of balanced individuals. Such a step from the colleges and schools encourages the students to take up the cause of social work and eradicate evils from the society.

It is true that each individual cannot become a social worker, or is not able to join a social service institute, but we can do our little bit by following the path taught in colleges. Respecting the importance of public property and engaging in a little social work makes a person more conscientious and dutiful towards the society. These values surely go a long way in developing a balanced and all around personality of a person.

Below we have included some example issue topics. These are exercises for you to complete, think about the way that they're graded, plan your time, and get somebody to score them for you!

Here are some examples of the type of issue essay prompts that you could expect on the day, read them and notice similarities and differences, and then when you're ready, start answering some.

Important truths begin as outrageous, or at least uncomfortable, attacks upon the accepted wisdom of the time.

Directions: Write a response in which you discuss the extent to which you agree or disagree with the claim. In developing and supporting your position, be sure to address the most compelling reasons and/or examples that could be used to challenge your position. Use the space below to plan your essay, and write your essay on lined paper. File your essays, and look back through your plans to assess your progress as you get used to the format of the essays.

Originality does not mean thinking something that was never thought before, it means putting old ideas together in new ways....

Directions: *Write a response in which you discuss the extent to which you agree or disagree with the claim. In developing and supporting your position, be sure to address the most compelling reasons and/or examples that could be used to challenge your position. Use the space below to plan your essay, and write your essay on lined paper. File your essays, and look back through your plans to assess your progress as you get used to the format of the essays.*

Laws should not be rigid or fixed. Instead, they should be flexible enough to take account of various circumstances, times, and places.

Directions: Write a response in which you discuss the extent to which you agree or disagree with the claim. In developing and supporting your position, be sure to address the most compelling reasons and/or examples that could be used to challenge your position. Use the space below to plan your essay, and write your essay on lined paper. File your essays, and look back through your plans to assess your progress as you get used to the format of the essays.

GRE® Argument Essay Example

The GRE® Argument Writing task is designed to test your ability to your critical-reasoning and analytic (as well as writing) skills. Your task is to compose an essay in which you provide a focused critique of the stated argument — but not to present your own views on the argument's topic.

The following GRE®-style Argument prompt consists of an argument followed by a directive for responding to the argument. Keep in mind: the argument itself is not from the official pool, and so you won't see this one on the actual GRE®.

GRE® Argument Prompt

The following appeared in the editorial column of the Fern County Gazette newspaper:

The Fern County Council made the right decision when it unanimously voted to convert the Northside branch of the county library system into a computer-skills training facility for public use. The converted facility will fill what is certain, based on national trends, to be a growing need among county residents for training in computer skills. And since our library system boasts more volumes per resident than any other system in the state, the remaining branches will adequately serve the future needs of Fern County residents.

Discuss what evidence you would need to properly evaluate the argument, and explain how that evidence might strengthen or weaken the argument.

Following is a sample essay that responds to the above prompt. As you read the essay, keep in mind:

Each of the three body paragraphs identifies a different aspect of the argument, discusses what additional evidence is needed to properly evaluate that aspect, and explains how that evidence might bear on the argument.

This essay is brief enough to plan and type in 30 minutes. The essay is intended as a benchmark response — one that would earn a top score of 6. But it is by no means "the" correct response to the prompt. Other top-scoring essays might be organized differently, or make different points.

Example resonse

This editorial argues that the Fern County Council's decision to convert a library branch to a computer-skills training facility was the "right" one. However, its author fails to provide sufficient information to permit a proper evaluation of the argument's reasoning. Each point of deficiency is discussed separately below.

One of the argument's deficiencies involves the claim, based on a national trend, that there is "certain" to be a growing need in Fern County for computer-skills training. The author provides no specific evidence that the county conforms to the cited trend. Lacking such evidence, it is entirely possible that the Fern County residents are, by and large, already highly proficient in using computers. Of course, it is also possible that a large and growing segment of the local population consists of senior citizens and/or young children — two groups who typically need computer-skills training — or unemployed workers needing to learn computer skills in order to find jobs. In any event, more information about the county's current and anticipated demographics is needed in order

to determine the extent to which Fern County residents actually need and would use the Northside computer-training facility.

Another of the argument's deficiencies is that it provides no information about alternative means of providing computer-skills training to county residents. Perhaps certain local businesses or schools already provide computer-training facilities and services to the general public — in which case it would be useful to know whether those alternatives are affordable for most county residents and whether they suffice to meet anticipated demand. Or perhaps county residents are for the most part willing to teach themselves computer skills at home using books, DVDs and online tutorials — in which case it would be helpful to know the extent to which affordable broadband Internet access is available to Fern County households. If it turns out that county residents can easily obtain computer-skills training through means such as these, converting the Northside branch might not have been a sensible idea.

Yet another of the editorial's shortcomings has to do with the number of books in the Fern County library system. The mere fact that the system boasts a great number of books per capita does not necessarily mean that the supply is adequate or that it will be adequate in the future. A full assessment of whether the remaining branches provide adequate shelf space and/or printed materials would require detailed information about the library system's inventory vis-à-vis the current and anticipated needs and interests of Fern County residents. If more, or more types, of printed books and periodicals are needed, then it would appear in retrospect that converting the Northside branch to a computer training center was a bad idea.

In a nutshell, then, a proper evaluation of the editorial requires more information about current as well as anticipated demand for computer-skills training in Fern County and about the adequacy of the library system's stacks to meet the interests and preferences of the county's residents.

Now, we have included some example argument topics. Like the Issue Topics, these are exercises for you to complete, think about the way that they're graded, plan your time, and get somebody to score them for you!

A company called wet weather investments specialize in providing major investment advice to customers. On a recent blog post they wrote:

"Homes in the North USA, where winters are typically cold, have traditionally used oil as their major fuel for heating. Last year that region experienced thirty days with below-average temperatures, and local weather forecasters throughout the region predict that this weather pattern will continue for several more years. Furthermore, many new homes have been built in this region during the past year. Because of these developments, we predict an increased demand for heating oil and recommend major investment in Mega Oil Inc. one of whose major business operations is the retail sale of home heating oil."

Directions: Write a response in which you discuss what specific evidence is needed to evaluate the argument and explain how the evidence would weaken or strengthen the argument. Use the space below to plan your essay, and write your essay on lined paper. File your essays, and look back through your plans to assess your progress as you get used to the format of the essays.

On a website of 93.6 ZAS FM radio station, the owner wrote:

"To reverse a decline in listener numbers, our owners have decided that 93.6 ZAS FM must change from its current jazz-music format. The decline has occurred despite population growth in our listening area, but that growth has resulted mainly from people moving here after their retirement. We must make listeners of these new residents. We could switch to a music format tailored to their tastes, but a continuing decline in local sales of recorded music suggests limited interest in music. Instead we should change to a news and talk format, a form of radio that is increasingly popular in our area."

Directions: *Write a response in which you discuss what specific evidence is needed to evaluate the argument and explain how the evidence would weaken or strengthen the argument. Use the space below to plan your essay, and write your essay on lined paper. File your essays, and look back through your plans to assess your progress as you get used to the format of the essays.*

Three years ago, because of flooding at the Western Palean Wildlife Preserve, 100 lions and 100 western gazelles were moved to the East Palean Preserve, an area that is home to most of the same species that are found in the western preserve, though in larger numbers, and to the eastern gazelle, a close relative of the western gazelle. The only difference in climate is that the eastern preserve typically has slightly less rainfall. Unfortunately, after three years in the eastern preserve, the imported western gazelle population has been virtually eliminated. Since the slight reduction in rainfall cannot be the cause of the virtual elimination of western gazelle, their disappearance must have been caused by the larger number of predators in the eastern preserve.

Directions: Write a response in which you discuss what specific evidence is needed to evaluate the argument and explain how the evidence would weaken or strengthen the argument. Use the space below to plan your essay, and write your essay on lined paper. File your essays, and look back through your plans to assess your progress as you get used to the format of the essays.

Ok, so now that you have read our guide and practiced the skills and techniques advised, take a break and allocate some time to properly sit the following practice tests. Good luck!

Practice Test 1

Section 1: Issue Topic

Parenting ability can be measured by how successful a child grows up to be.

Allotted Time: *30 minutes*

Directions: *Write a response in which you discuss the extent to which you agree or disagree with the claim. In developing and supporting your position, be sure to address the most compelling reasons and/or examples that could be used to challenge your position.*

The quality of your answer will be assessed based on your ability to do the following:

- *Respond to the specific task instructions.*

- *Consider the complexities of the issue.*

- *Organize, develop, and express your ideas.*

- *Support your ideas with relevant reasons and/or examples.*

- *Control the elements of standard English.*

Section 2: Argument Topic

Recent analysis of crime data in Banstoble City revealed that the most common crimes are criminal damage, home invasion and burglary. Moreover, the vast majority of these crimes occur between the hours of 9pm and 4 am. Hence, Banstoble's police chief has decided to increase the number of police officers patrolling residential areas during these times in order to decrease the overall crime rate in the city. Additionally, a specialist response team will be created to investigate incidences of criminal damage, home invasion and burglary with a view to catching repeat offenders. The police chief is confident that these initiatives will work and lead to Banstoble becoming a safer city.

Allotted Time: *30 minutes*

Directions: *Write a response in which you discuss the questions that would need to be answered in order to decide whether the recommendation or argument detailed above is reasonable. Ensure that you explain how the answers to these questions would help to evaluate the recommendation or argument.*

The quality of your answer will be assessed based on your ability to do the following:

- *Respond to the specific task instructions.*

- *Identify and analyse features of the argument relevant to the assigned task.*

- *Organise, develop and express your ideas.*

- *Support your analysis with relevant reasons and/or examples.*

- *Control the elements of standard written English.*

Section 3: Quantitative Reasoning

Allotted Time: 35 minutes

Number of Questions: 20 questions

1. $3x - 4y = -12$

   $6x + 2y = 36$

Quantity A	Quantity B
x	y

   A. Quantity A is greater

   B. Quantity B is greater

   C. The two quantities are equal

   D. The relationship cannot be determined from the information given

2. A scout's uniform features square, triangular and circular badges. One quarter of the badges are square. One third of the remaining badges are triangular.

Quantity A	Quantity B
The number of square badges	The number of triangular badges

   A. Quantity A is greater

   B. Quantity B is greater

   C. The two quantities are equal

   D. The relationship cannot be determined from the information given

3.

Quantity A	Quantity B
$xy + 2$	$(x + 7)(y - 3)$

   A. Quantity A is greater

   B. Quantity B is greater

   C. The two quantities are equal

   D. The relationship cannot be determined from the information given

4. $y = (23)(24)(25)(26)(27)$

Quantity A	Quantity B
The units digit	0

A.   Quantity A is greater

B.   Quantity B is greater

C.   The two quantities are equal

D.   The relationship cannot be determined from the information given

5.   Eric, Alan and Dave are all fishermen. Eric typically catches three times as many fish as Alan each day. Over the course of two days, Dave typically catches as many fish as Alan catches in five days.

Quantity A	Quantity B
The number of fish Eric typically catches each day.	The number of fish Dave typically catches each day.

A.   Quantity A is greater

B.   Quantity B is greater

C.   The two quantities are equal

D.   The relationship cannot be determined from the information given

6.   The nets for a cube and a cuboid are shown with their dimensions. They are not drawn to scale.

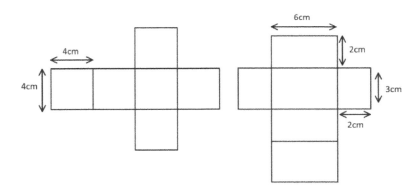

Quantity A	Quantity B
The surface area of the cube.	The surface area of the cuboid.

A.   Quantity A is greater

B.   Quantity B is greater

C.   The two quantities are equal

D. The relationship cannot be determined from the information given

7. a = b + 1 and 5 < ab < 8

| Quantity A | Quantity B |
| $2a + b^2$ | $a^2 + 2b$ |

A. Quantity A is greater

B. Quantity B is greater

C. The two quantities are equal

D. The relationship cannot be determined from the information given

8. Lines AB and CD are parallel. Find the angle marked x.

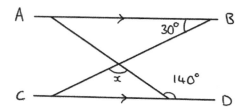

A. 100°

B. 110°

C. 105°

D. 120°

E. 130°

9. Mary has four shelves in her room; each shelf can fit one trophy. Mary has recently won 10 trophies. How many ways can she arrange her new trophies?

A. 55

B. 1000

C. 2456

D. 3030

E. 5040

10. Seven friends want to play battleships. Each game of battle ships requires two players. How many games have to be played to ensure that every player plays every other player?

A. 14

B. 15

C. 18

D. 21

E. 25

11. A burger restaurant employs 3 chefs during the week. These 3 chefs can make a total of 225 burgers in 5 hours. On the weekends, the restaurant employs more chefs. With all the chefs working on the weekends, 750 burgers can be made in 10 hours. How many more chefs are working on the weekend compared to in the week?

A. 5

B. 4

C. 3

D. 2

E. 1

12. If x is a positive integer, which expression below gives the number of integers that are greater than 3x + 1 and smaller than 4x + 3?

A. 3x - 2

B. x + 1

C. 4x + 1

D. x + 3

E. x

13. If $2 < y < 8$, $4 < x < 7$ and $z = \dfrac{2x}{y}$. Which of the following values could z be equal to?

A. 7

B. 1

C. 6

D. 5

E. 0

14. If $x^2 - 9 = 0$, $x^2 + xy - 18 = 0$ and x and y are both positive integers, what are the values of x and y?

A. x = 2, y = 1

B. x = 3, y = 1

C. x = 1, y = 3

D. x = 1, y = 2

E. x = 3, y = 3

15. If 4 < a < 8 and -3 < b < -1, indicate all of the following expressions that must be true.

A. a + b > 0

B. a - b > 0

C. b - a > 0

D. b - a < 0

E. 2b + a < 0

16. The square ABCD has a perimeter of 36 cm. Point E lies exactly in the center of square ABCD. What is the area of triangle DEC?

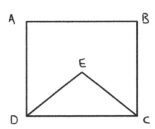

A. 64 cm²

B. 32 cm²

C. 16 cm²

D. 8 cm²

E. 4 cm²

17. A car garage employs 3 mechanics. Three mechanics are able to fully service 6 cars in 4 hours. If the car garage doubled its number of mechanics, how long would it take for the garage to fully service 15 cars?

A. 5 hours

B. 4 hours

C. 6 hours

D. 6.5 hours

E. 8 hours

The graph shows the number of male and female students who achieved each grade in a mathematics exam. And refers to questions 18-20:

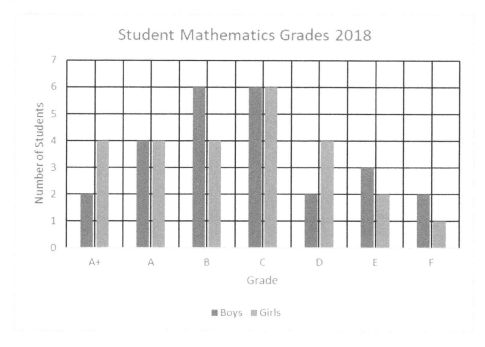

18. For which grade was the ratio of boys to girls the greatest?

   A. A+

   B. B

   C. D

   D. E

   E. F

19. What percentage of students achieved a B or above?

   A. 4%

   B. 12%

   C. 30%

   D. 48%

   E. 58%

20. Grades A and A+ are considered to be 'outstanding'. How many students would need to improve their grades for the school to declare that "50% of the students achieve outstanding results"?

A. 4

B. 8

C. 11

D. 15

E. 20

Section 4: Verbal Reasoning

Allotted Time: 30 minutes

Number of Questions: 20 questions

Text Completion

Directions: Each of the passages below has had one, two or three words omitted. For each of the blacks, select a word that best fits the meaning of the sentence and passage. If more than one word has been omitted, each blank will have its own set of words to choose from. This is indicated by (i), (ii) and (iii).

Sentence Equivalence

Directions: For each of the following sentences below, select two words from the list which, when inserted into the sentence, are grammatically correct and produce two sentences of similar meaning.

Reading Comprehension

Directions: Each passage in this group is followed by questions based on its content. After reading a passage, choose the best answer to each question. Answer all questions following a passage on the basis of what is stated or implied in that passage.

1. With shifts in global power dynamics and the future of the Global Democratic Order uncertain, the quest for chemical disarmament has become even more _____.

    A. insipid

    B. exigent

    C. salubrious

    D. penurious

    E. facile

2. The political strategy of a demagogue involves appealing to the desires and fears of the _____.

    A. potentate

    B. justiciar

    C. fraternity

    D. prophylactic

    E. canaille

3. The twelve-year old took to the stage with such _____ that the audience were convinced of his future stardom.

    A. aplomb

    B. degradation

    C. anticity

    D. indemnity

    E. plumage

4. The *Atrahasis* text returns repeatedly to the division of the cosmos into three parts given over to different gods. Anu receives (i) _____ over the sky, Enlil governs the wind and Enki rules the waves. Burkert argues that Poseidon's speech in the *Iliad* on the division of the cosmos between the three chief male deities is so similar to the system in the *Atrahasis* that Eastern tradition must have (ii) _____ the Greek one.

Blank (i)	Blank (ii)
counterfactual	influenced
dominion	stymied
vivacious	evaded

5. The term sexual selection was (i) _____ by Darwin to explain the presence of ornaments in males that seemed (ii) _____ as an adaptation to the environment. Today it is described as the selection caused by the ability of some individuals of a population to reproduce more frequently or with higher fitness mates than other members of the population.

Blank (i)	Blank (ii)
cordial	cumbersome
garrulous	inexplicable
coined	partisan

6. With the rise of nationalism in the Western world, the Liberal Democratic Order is (i) _____. President Trump, who (ii) _____ promotes America's interests above all else, has been a vocal critic of globalisation and (iii) _____ an isolationist foreign policy. He has gone as far as to suggest that allied nations who seek American support should be prepared to compensate the United States for economic costs.

Blank (i)	Blank (ii)	Blank (iii)

somatic	incredulously	espouses
fragmenting	posthumously	dislodges
perfunctory	unreservedly	edifies

7. Alan Ericson's commitment to the animal rights movement was _____.

   A. immutable

   B. infallible

   C. uncompromising

   D. nocturnal

   E. ebullient

   F. defamatory

8. For decades, students have been both fascinated and completely _____ by Schrodinger's equation.
   A. coddled

   B. stipulated

   C. imbued

   D. dumfounded

   E. perplexed

   F. beguiled

9. Teachers needs to recognise how _____ technology is in the life of teenagers.

   A. nebulous

   B. pervasive

   C. oblivious

   D. ubiquitous

   E. arboreal

   F. fallacious

10. The king will always be remembered and revered for his _____ rule.

   A. whimsical

   B. indomitable

C. perspicacious

D. sagacious

E. grandiloquent

F. transient

11. Two extremes dominate the depiction of kangaroos in popular culture. The first extreme is a dangerous and unpredictable animal, prepared to go toe-to-toe with any human. The other extreme shows kangaroos to be gentle and mothering – these depictions often include a mother with their young _____ in their pouch.

A. dislodged

B. stifled

C. nestled

D. castigated

E. ensconced

F. cajoled

12. Furthermore, the inclusion of such _____ symbolism demonstrates Gide's determination to prioritise his aesthetic aims over verisimilitude.

A. feckless

B. evocative

C. hegemonic

D. poignant

E. sycophantic

F. urbane

Questions 13-16 refers to the following passage:

Caesar faced many problems in 46-45 BC. He had lost many men to civil war; the survivors had lost money in ruinous taxes and had their property looted and destroyed and the victorious soldiery were clamouring for their reward. The threat of Pompey loomed from Spain and there was a great need for a strong leader to breathe life into the dying Republic. Therefore, Caesar had to combine his aims for his own political advancement with new aims to rebuild the Republic in such a way that it would not infringe upon his autocratic designs. In assessing the extent to which these aims were reasonable, we ought to examine Caesar's political aims both within the context

of the ideology of the Republic and the condition of the Republic before assessing whether his plans for Rome which were halted by his assassination were viable and in the interests of the Republic.

13. The passage is primarily concerned with:

    A. Describing why Pompey was a threat to Rome.

    B. Criticizing scholars who ignore the state that the Roman Republic was in when assessing Caesar's political decisions.

    C. Explaining that Caesar's politics can be understood by considering both his political ideology and the wider context of his rule in this period.

    D. Discussing the reasons behind Caesar's assassination.

    E. Identifying the problems faced by Caesar during his rule.

14. The phrase 'breathe life into' most nearly means:

    A. Emulate

    B. Disseminate

    C. Revive

    D. Hinder

    E. Obviate

15. Based on the passage, the state of the Roman Republic at this time could be described as:

    A. In tatters

    B. Thriving

    C. Up and coming

    D. Trail blazing

    E. Unknown

16. It can be inferred from this passage, that Caesar was:

    A. A benevolent leader who had the best interests of his people at heart.

    B. Concerned primarily with amassing and consolidating power.

    C. Acutely aware of ongoing schemes to overthrow him.

    D. An incapable leader who had created many problems in Rome.

    E. Determined to relieve the tax burden on survivors of the civil war.

Questions 17-20 refers to the following passage:

Speciation is where one species becomes two distinct species as a result of divergence and subsequent reproductive isolation. Speciation can arise from a number of micro-evolutionary processes that fall into one of two categories; sexual selection and ecological selection. Ecological speciation occurs when populations diverge into reproductively isolated groups due to differences in ecological traits. The agents of ecological speciation are always extrinsic, i.e. not intraspecific factors. These factors include but are not limited to food, range, habitat, interspecific competition and predation. Conversely, sexual selection driven speciation occurs when episodes of male-female co-evolution occur independently and simultaneously resulting in a divergence in sexual choice within a population. Sexual selection can also accelerate ecological speciation as ecologically distinct populations diverge in their sexual preferences. Both ecological and sexual speciation have, over the years, been argued to play important roles in speciation.

17. What is the purpose of the highlighted sentence?

   A. For the writer to demonstrate their understanding of this phenomenon.

   B. For the writer to establish academic authority.

   C. To explaining the factors affecting a scientific phenomenon.

   D. To define a scientific term exactly for the reader's understanding.

   E. To emphasise the importance of understanding this phenomenon.

18. Which of the following can be inferred from the passage? Select all that apply.

   A. Sexual selection and ecological selection are distinct and completely independent.

   B. Sexual selection can affect ecological selection.

   C. Ecological selection can affect sexual selection.

   D. Sexual selection and ecological selection are the same thing.

   E. Sexual selection and ecological selection are not fully understood.

19. Which of the following would the author most likely consider to be an 'agent of ecological speciation'?

   A. Variations in the patterns of giraffe's spots.

   B. Rising water temperatures in the habitat of stickleback fish.

   C. The pack behaviour of wolves.

   D. Selective breeding of pedigree dogs

   E. The extinction of the dodo bird.

20. In the context of this passage, the words 'extrinsic' and 'interspecific' refer to:

    A. Types of speciation

    B. Types of animals

    C. Categorisations of factors

    D. Categorisations of animal traits

    E. Different sexual preferences

Section 5: Quantitative Reasoning

Allotted Time: 35 minutes

Number of Questions: 20 questions

1. $y = 1234 \times 5 \times 3 \times 3 + 3$

Quantity A	Quantity B
The units digit of y	3

A. Quantity A is greater

B. Quantity B is greater

C. The two quantities are equal

D. The relationship cannot be determined from the information given

2. $f(x) = x^2 + 3x + 2$

Quantity A	Quantity B
$f\left(\frac{1}{4}\right)$	3

A. Quantity A is greater

B. Quantity B is greater

C. The two quantities are equal

D. The relationship cannot be determined from the information given

3. $4x - 3y = 3$ and $x + y = 6$

Quantity A	Quantity B
x	y

A. Quantity A is greater

B. Quantity B is greater

C. The two quantities are equal

D. The relationship cannot be determined from the information given

4. Isiah has $20,000 in his bank. The interest rate in the first year was 15%. In the second year, the interest rate dropped to 14%.

Quantity A	Quantity B
The amount of money Isiah made through interest in the first year.	The amount of money Isiah made through interest in the second year.

A. Quantity A is greater

B. Quantity B is greater

C. The two quantities are equal

D. The relationship cannot be determined from the information given

5. Line EF is parallel with line HG. Line AB is parallel with line CD.

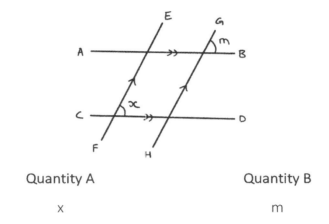

Quantity A	Quantity B
x	m

A. Quantity A is greater

B. Quantity B is greater

C. The two quantities are equal

D. The relationship cannot be determined from the information given

6. Ella and Martha are driving from town A to town B. For the first 30 miles Ella drives at 60 miles per hour but slows down to 45 miles per hour for the final 15 miles. Martha takes the same route but maintains a constant speed of 50 miles per hour.

Quantity A	Quantity B
The time taken for Ella to drive from town A to town B.	The time taken for Martha to travel from town A to town B.

A. Quantity A is greater

B. Quantity B is greater

C. The two quantities are equal

D.   The relationship cannot be determined from the information given

7.   Two right angled triangles are shown.

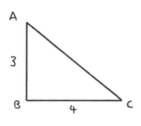 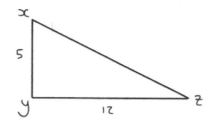

Note: Figure not drawn on the scale

Quantity A	Quantity B
3 x AC	XZ

A.   Quantity A is greater

B.   Quantity B is greater

C.   The two quantities are equal

D.   The relationship cannot be determined from the information given

8.   A four digit number is selected completely at random.

Quantity A	Quantity B
The probability that the units digit will be a prime number.	The probability that the units digit will no be a prime number.

A.   Quantity A is greater

B.   Quantity B is greater

C.   The two quantities are equal

D.   The relationship cannot be determined from the information given

9. $2^3 \times 3^X \times 4 = 6 \times 12^2$. Find x.

A.   1

B.   2

C.   3

D.   4

E.   5

10. A square can be drawn to connect the center of four circles (as shown). If the area of the square is 36, what is the total area of the circles in terms of π?

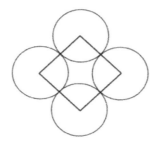

    A. 12π

    B. 36π

    C. 72π

    D. 144π

    E. 288π

11. $\dfrac{x + 2y}{x} = 5\dfrac{2}{3}$. Find $\dfrac{y}{x}$.

    A. $\dfrac{3}{7}$

    B. $\dfrac{2}{5}$

    C. $\dfrac{7}{5}$

    D. $\dfrac{7}{3}$

    E. $\dfrac{1}{3}$

12. $6.0 \times 10^{-2} + 7.0 \times 10^{-3} + 0.7 \times 10^{-2}$

Which of the following values is equal to the expression above?

    A. 7.4×10^{-3}

    B. 7.4×10^{-2}

    C. 7.4×10^{-1}

    D. 0.74×10^{-4}

    E. 0.74

13. Use the axes to determine the total area covered by the shapes shown.

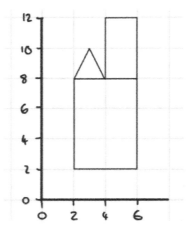

A. 24

B. 28

C. 30

D. 32

E. 34

14. Alice can't remember her 4 digit pin number. She knows that it only contains digits 0-6 inclusive. How many possible pin numbers can be made from these digits?

A. 200

B. 360

C. 400

D. 460

E. 500

15. If a, b and c sum to 13, 2b - a = 1 and 2c + b = 8, what is the value of ac?

A. 2

B. 6

C. 10

D. 14

E. 15

16. ABDE is a square. C is exactly at the midpoint of line BD. Given that the length of AC is 4√5, find the length of one side of the square.

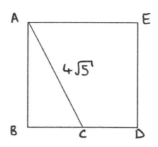

A. 4

B. 5

C. 6

D. 7

E. 8

17. Find the point at which the lines y = x + 2 and y = -4x + 2 intersect.

A. (3,9)

B. (0,2)

C. (2,4)

D. (-1,3)

E. (0,4)

The graph shows the results of a random sample of 7 students were asked to provide their weekly earnings and weekly expenditure. And refers to questions 18-20:

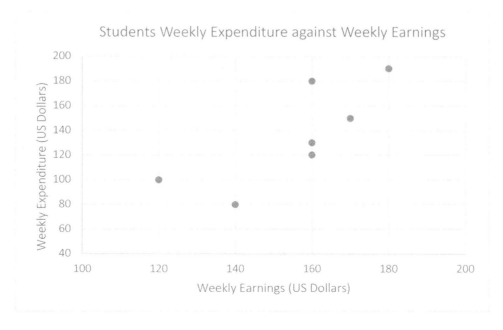

18. How many students spent less than they earned each week?

    A. 1

    B. 2

    C. 3

    D. 4

    E. 5

19. How many students spent more than 70% of their earnings each week?

    A. 3

    B. 4

    C. 5

    D. 6

    E. 7

20. If every student in the sample received a 10% pay rise, what would the new range of weekly earnings be among the sample?

    A. 88

    B. 93

    C. 105

    D. 120

    E. 125

Section 6: Verbal Reasoning

Allotted Time: 30 minutes

Number of Questions: 20 questions

Text Completion

Directions: Each of the passages below has had one, two or three words omitted. For each of the blacks, select a word that best fits the meaning of the sentence and passage. If more than one word has been omitted, each blank will have its own set of words to choose from. This is indicated by (i), (ii) and (iii).

Sentence Equivalence

Directions: For each of the following sentences below, select two words from the list which, when inserted into the sentence, are grammatically correct and produce two sentences of similar meaning.

Reading Comprehension

Directions: Each passage in this group is followed by questions based on its content. After reading a passage, choose the best answer to each question. Answer all questions following a passage on the basis of what is stated or implied in that passage.

1. With little to add variability to the _____ daily routine, schooling quickly became monotonous.

   A. shrill

   B. quotidian

   C. tenuous

   D. hauteur

   E. rapacious

2. It is widely accepted in labour economics that educated individuals and their families experience numerous private non-market benefits; they include a more _____ life, higher social status and more stable marriages.

   A. fervid

   B. baleful

   C. fetid

   D. salubrious

   E. contrarious

3. An _____ problem present throughout the literature is how to define 'poverty'. Many scholars concur that poverty is not simply quantified in the monetary sense; there is also social poverty, poverty of opportunity etc.

   A. contrite

   B. palliative

   C. enduring

   D. pragmatic

   E. demonstrative

4. Before discussing whether the (i) _____ of chastity was used as a tool to control women in Rome, it is (ii) _____ to first consider whether the Vestals were required to be virgins in the strictest physical sense.

Blank (i)	Blank (ii)
notion	onerous
epilogue	malicious
morose	prudent

5. Parliamentary elections are (i) _____ and sensitive times in every country and restricting the flow of information to the general populous (ii) _____ the democratic process.

Blank (i)	Blank (ii)
noxious	disparate
polemic	engender
contentious	compromises

6. Peer mentorship is rarely (i) _____, it is more often reciprocal. The mentee benefits from the lived experience of the mentor, which can often provide more useful and (ii) _____ guidance than traditional training or induction programs. The mentor, although more experienced, can still learn from the mentee. The mentee comes with different experiences and new (iii) _____ which can prompt the mentor to reflect on their own practices and consider new approaches to their work. It is the opportunity for reciprocal learning that is the most unique and successful aspect of peer mentorship.

Blank (i)	Blank (ii)	Blank (iii)
banal	endemic	perspectives

unidirectional	trivial	modalities
putative	nuanced	cynicisms

7. Persistence is crucial in journalism; to succeed, one needs to show themselves to be _____.

    A. indefatigable

    B. doleful

    C. unrelenting

    D. unenviable

    E. intractable

    F. laconic

8. As the daughter of a diplomat, the importance of etiquette was impressed upon Eleanor from a young age. Consequently, Eleanor was often disgusted, or even outraged by her nephew's _____.

    A. gaucherie

    B. anguish

    C. divergence

    D. moderation

    E. volatility

    F. indecorum

Questions 9-12 refers to the following passage:

Audiobook sales have doubled in the last five years while print and e-book sales are flat. These trends might lead us to fear that audiobooks will do to reading what keyboarding has done to handwriting — rendered it a skill that seems quaint and whose value is open to debate. But examining how we read and how we listen shows that each is best suited to different purposes, and neither is superior. In fact, they overlap considerably. Consider why audiobooks are a good workaround for people with dyslexia: they allow listeners to get the meaning while skirting the work of decoding, that is, the translation of print on the page to words in the mind. Although decoding is serious work for beginning readers, it's automatic by high school, and no more effortful or error prone than listening. Once you've identified the words (whether by listening or reading), the same mental process comprehends the sentences and paragraphs they form. Writing is less than 6,000 years old, insufficient time for the evolution of specialized mental processes devoted to reading. We use the mental mechanism that evolved to understand oral language to support the comprehension of written language. Indeed, research shows that adults get nearly identical scores on a reading test if they listen to the passages instead of reading them.

9. The two highlighted sentences above serve what purpose in this passage?

    A. The first sentence suggests a possible position that one might adopt. The second sentence explains why this position is misguided.

    B. The first sentence provides support for a position. The second sentence further supports this position.

    C. The first sentence summarises the main argument of the passage. The second sentence provides an example to support the main argument.

    D. The first sentence states the conclusion of the passage. The second sentence provides support for this conclusion.

    E. The first sentence outlines an argument. The second sentence refutes this argument.

10. According to the passage:

    A. Audiobooks will replace reading.

    B. Audiobooks will never replace reading.

    C. Audiobooks are used in different way and in different circumstances than books.

    D. Audiobooks are superior to books.

    E. People do not enjoy reading as much as they enjoy listening to audiobooks.

11. The author references scientific studies in order to:

    A. Refute a counter argument.

    B. Provide evidence for his main point.

    C. Provide an illustrative example.

    D. Explain a complex idea.

    E. Establish himself as an expert.

12. Select all that apply. According to the author, individuals who have dyslexia, find the process of decoding written text:

    A. Insipid

    B. Dull

    C. Challenging

    D. Arduous

    E. Scintillating

INNOTI N
ACADEMIC PREP

Questions 13-16 refers to the following passage:

Private schooling has inequality as a founding premise – with entry almost entirely dependent on the ability of parents to pay. Private schools perpetuate inequalities and maintain privilege. This can be seen in the over-representation of privately educated people in better universities, and in key professional careers that shape society – such as journalism, law, politics and finance. This dominance is achieved not only through the educational outcomes produced by the schools in terms of qualifications but also through what sociologists regard as the social and cultural capital that can be gained in private schools. In this way, attending a private school gives students a ready-made network of similarly advantaged friends to help them in the future. And pupils will also have learned ways of "being" and interacting, which can help ease the way through interviews for university, professional training and jobs. The "old boys" or "old girls" networks thrive on a sense of entitlement, belonging and common cultural references.

13. Judging from this passage, which of the following statements would the author most agree with?

    A. Private school pupils tend to have more successful careers primarily because they achieve higher grades in school.

    B. If non-private school pupils are to compete with private school pupils in the job market, they need to make connections with more influential people.

    C. The social networks and connections of privately educated individuals helps to propel them in their careers and leads to overrepresentation of privately educated students in the top jobs.

    D. Private school students tend to work harder in school, which results in them achieving higher grades.

    E. State-run schools (i.e. non-private) cannot compete academically with private schools.

14. What is the purpose of the two highlighted sentences?

    A. The first highlighted sentence states the authors argument and the second highlighted sentence refutes existing counter arguments.

    B. Both sentences present evidence to support the authors main argument.

    C. The first highlighted sentence explains the authors main argument and the second highlighted sentence presents evidence to support this argument.

    D. The first highlighted sentence presents a problem and the second highlighted sentence presents the solution.

    E. The first highlighted sentence presents the main point of the passage and the second highlighted sentence summarises the authors argument.

15. The phrase 'social capital', in this context, most closely means:

A. Nepotism

B. The value that being part of a certain social group can bring to an individual.

C. Fellowship

D. The group of friends an individual considers themselves most close to.

E. The sense of belonging that comes from social networks.

16. Which of the following can be inferred from the passage?

A. Private school students do not deserve places at the top universities.

B. Privately educated students have more opportunities to influence society in later life.

C. Private schools should be abolished.

D. Private schools should offer scholarships to poor students.

E. There is no way to address the inequalities that the private education system presents.

Questions 17-20 refers to the following passage:

As I applied so closely, it may be easily conceived that my progress was rapid. My ardour was indeed the astonishment of the students, and my proficiency that of the masters. Professor Krempe often asked me, with a sly smile, how Cornelius Agrippa went on, whilst M. Waldman expressed the most heartfelt exultation in my progress. Two years passed in this manner, during which I paid no visit to Geneva, but was engaged, heart and soul, in the pursuit of some discoveries which I hoped to make. None but those who have experienced them can conceive of the enticements of science. In other studies you go as far as others have gone before you, and there is nothing more to know; but in a scientific pursuit there is continual food for discovery and wonder. A mind of moderate capacity which closely pursues one study must infallibly arrive at great proficiency in that study; and I, who continually sought the attainment of one object of pursuit and was solely wrapped up in this, improved so rapidly that at the end of two years I made some discoveries in the improvement of some chemical instruments, which procured me great esteem and admiration at the university. When I had arrived at this point and had become as well acquainted with the theory and practice of natural philosophy as depended on the lessons of any of the professors at Ingolstadt, my residence there being no longer conducive to my improvements, I thought of returning to my friends and my native town, when an incident happened that protracted my stay.

17. The main purpose of this passage is:

A. To describe the author's experience of studying at university.

B. To encourage others to study science.

C. To argue why science should be studied at university.

D. To praise the author's predecessors for their great teaching.

E. To explain a particular scientific phenomenon.

18. The author enjoys the study of science over other subjects because:

    A. Science is more complex than other subjects.

    B. Studying science allows students more freedom to explore.

    C. Studying science is prescriptive.

    D. Studying science involves discovery, and for that reason, it is the most engaging subject.

    E. Studying science is filled with uncertainty and unpredictability.

19. The purpose of the highlighted sentence is to:

    A. Introduce new characters.

    B. Illustrate how capable the author is in the sciences.

    C. Explain why the author chose to write the passage.

    D. Clarify a misconception that the reader may have.

    E. Provide evidence for the authors argument.

20. Based on the passage, which of the following words could be used to describe the main character?

    A. Embattled

    B. Diligent

    C. Inquisitive

    D. Ebullient

    E. Enigmatic

Answers

Section 1: Issue Topic

Compare your response to the advice in the analytical writing area to calculate your score.

Section 2: Argument Topic

Compare your response to the advice in the analytical writing area to calculate your score.

Section 3: Quantitative Reasoning

1. B

2. C

3. D

4. C

5. A

6. A

7. D

8. B

9. E

10. D

11. D

12. B

13. C and D

14. B

15. A, B and D

16. C

17. A

18. E

19. D

20. C

Section 4: Verbal Reasoning

1. (B) exigent

2. (E) canaille

3. (A) aplomb

4. (i) dominion (ii) influenced

5. (i) coined (ii) inexplicable

6. (i) fragmenting (ii) unreservedly (iii) espouses

7. (A) immutable (C) uncompromising

8. (D) dumfounded (E) perplexed

9. (B) pervasive (D) ubiquitous

10. (C) perspicacious (D) sagacious

11. (C) nestled (E) ensconced

12. (B) evocative (D) poignant

13. B

14. C

15. A

16. B

17. C

18. B

19. B

20. C

Section 5: Quantitative Reasoning

1. C

2. B

3. C

4. B

5. C

6. B

7. A

8. B

9. C

10. B

11. D

12. B

13. E

14. B

15. D

16. E

17. B

18. E

19. C

20. A

Section 6: Verbal Reasoning

1. (B) quotidian

2. (D) salubrious

3. (C) enduring

4. (i) notion (ii) prudent

5. (i) contentious (ii) compromises

6. (i) unidirectional (ii) nuanced (iii) perspectives

7. (A) indefatigable (C) unrelenting

8. (A) gaucherie (F) indecorum

9. A

10. C

11. B

12. C and D

13. C

14. E

15. B

16. C

17. A

18. D

19. B

20. B and C

Practice Test 2

Section 1: Issue Topic

The main purpose of imprisoning people to punish them for their crimes so that they are less likely to break the law in the future. Hence, imprisonment should not be a pleasant experience.

Allotted Time: 30 minutes

Directions: *Write a response in which you discuss the extent to which you agree or disagree with the claim. In developing and supporting your position, be sure to address the most compelling reasons and/or examples that could be used to challenge your position.*

The quality of your answer will be assessed based on your ability to do the following:

- *Respond to the specific task instructions.*

- *Consider the complexities of the issue.*

- *Organize, develop, and express your ideas.*

- *Support your ideas with relevant reasons and/or examples.*

- *Control the elements of standard English.*

Section 2: Argument Topic

The recruitment of teachers to rural areas is an ongoing problem in Gredonia. For decades, rural schools have struggled to attract trained teachers and, as a result, rural student exam scores have consistently been below their urban counterparts. In order to close this rural-urban educational divide, the Gredonian government have agreed to offer financial incentives for teachers to move to rural locations. Specifically, if a teacher moves to a rural school, they will receive a one-off payment equal to 20% of their salary. It is hoped that this financial incentive will attract qualified teachers to rural locations which will thereby improve the quality of rural education and boost academic attainment.

Allotted Time: *30 minutes*

Directions: *Write a response in which you discuss the questions that would need to be answered in order to decide whether the recommendation or argument detailed above is reasonable. Ensure that you explain how the answers to these questions would help to evaluate the recommendation or argument.*

The quality of your answer will be assessed based on your ability to do the following:

- *Respond to the specific task instructions.*

- *Identify and analyse features of the argument relevant to the assigned task.*

- *Organise, develop and express your ideas.*

- *Support your analysis with relevant reasons and/or examples.*

- *Control the elements of standard written English.*

Section 3: Quantitative Reasoning

Allotted Time: 35 minutes

Number of Questions: 20 questions

1. $7a - 3b = 26$
    $10a + 4b = 62$

Quantity A	Quantity B
a	b

    A. Quantity A is greater

    B. Quantity B is greater

    C. The two quantities are equal

    D. The relationship cannot be determined from the information given

2. A new design for a team flag features red, green and yellow stars. Half of the stars are green. One fifth of the remaining stars are yellow.

Quantity A	Quantity B
The number of red stars.	The number of green stars minus the number of yellow stars.

    A. Quantity A is greater

    B. Quantity B is greater

    C. The two quantities are equal

    D. The relationship cannot be determined from the information given

3.

Quantity A	Quantity B
$(x + 3)^2$	$x^2 + 21$

    A. Quantity A is greater

    B. Quantity B is greater

    C. The two quantities are equal

    D. The relationship cannot be determined from the information given

4. $y = (23)(24)(26)$

Quantity A	Quantity B
the tens digit	3

A. Quantity A is greater

B. Quantity B is greater

C. The two quantities are equal

D. The relationship cannot be determined from the information given

5. Each week, Ellen buys five times as many chocolate bars as Ruth and eats them all. Dora buys six times as many chocolate bars as Ruth each week, but always gives three chocolate bars away to friends and eats the rest.

Quantity A	Quantity B
The number of chocolate bars Ellen eats each week.	The number of chocolate bars Dora eats each week.

A. Quantity A is greater

B. Quantity B is greater

C. The two quantities are equal

D. The relationship cannot be determined from the information given

6. The net of a cuboid is shown. When the cuboid is assembled, it has a volume of 50 cm³

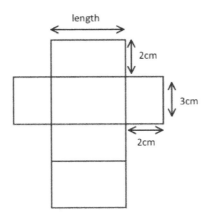

Quantity A	Quantity B
The length of the side labelled 'length'.	9 cm

A. Quantity A is greater

B. Quantity B is greater

C. The two quantities are equal

D. The relationship cannot be determined from the information given

7. $6 < ab < 9$ and $b = a - 6$

Quantity A	Quantity B
$a + b$	$a - b$

A. Quantity A is greater

B. Quantity B is greater

C. The two quantities are equal

D. The relationship cannot be determined from the information given

8. AED is an isosceles triangle, and ABCD is a parallelogram. Line AD is parallel with line BC and line AB is parallel with line DC. Find angle x.

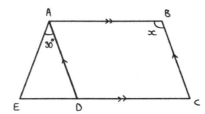

A. 95°

B. 100°

C. 105°

D. 110°

E. 120°

9. Xavier wants to give his new born daughter a name. He wants the name to only include the first 8 letters of the alphabet and he wants the name to be exactly three letters long. How many potential names can he choose from?

A. 8

B. 21

C. 62

D. 336

E. 876

10. A group of six friends want to enter a pub quiz tournament. Only four of them can be on the team. How many different combinations of the ten friends can be achieved?

    A. 14

    B. 15

    C. 18

    D. 21

    E. 25

11. The owner of a large coffee shop works out that with a team of 7 barristas, his shop can make 35 coffees in 15 minutes. If he sacks two of his barristas, how long will it take the shop to make 45 coffees?

    A. 27 minutes

    B. 30 minutes

    C. 35 minutes

    D. 33 minutes

    E. 42 minutes

12. If a is a positive integer, which expression below gives the number of integers that are greater than x - 1 but smaller than 2x + 2.

    A. x

    B. 2x - 1

    C. 2x + 1

    D. x - 1

    E. x + 2

13. If 3 < y < 10, 5 < x < 9 and z = 2xy, which of the following values could z be equal to?

    A. 20

    B. 100

    C. 150

    D. 180

    E. 200

14. What fraction of the circle shown is shaded yellow?

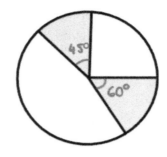

A. $\dfrac{1}{3}$

B. $\dfrac{1}{8}$

C. $\dfrac{2}{105}$

D. $\dfrac{3}{20}$

E. $\dfrac{7}{24}$

15. If $x^2 - 21x + 10 = 0$, what are the possible values for x?

A. 2, 1

B. 4, 3

C. 21, 1

D. 7, 3

E. 4, 2

16. If $2 < a < 5$ and $-2 < b < 2$, indicate all of the following expressions that must be true.

A. $a + b > -1$

B. $a - b > -1$

C. $b - a > 1$

D. $2b - a > 1$

E. $2b - 2a > 1$

17. Jack takes 2 hours to paint a room. When Jim helps him, it only takes 75 minutes to paint the room. How long would it take Jim to paint the room on his own?

   A. 2 hours

   B. 90 minutes

   C. 75 minutes

   D. 200 minutes

   E. 3 hours

The graph shows the results of a random sample of 7 students were asked to provide their weekly earnings and weekly expenditure. And refers to questions 18-20:

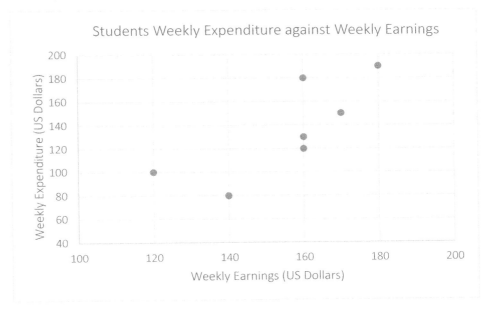

18. How many students spent more than they earned each week?

   A. 1

   B. 2

   C. 3

   D. 4

   E. 5

19. How many students spent more than 80% of their earnings each week?

   A. 3

   B. 4

C. 5

D. 6

E. 7

20. If every student in the sample received a 15% pay rise, what would the new range of weekly earnings be among the sample?

A. 52

B. 56

C. 65

D. 69

E. 82

Section 4: Verbal Reasoning

Allotted Time: 30 minutes

Number of Questions: 20 questions

Text Completion

Directions: Each of the passages below has had one, two or three words omitted. For each of the blacks, select a word that best fits the meaning of the sentence and passage. If more than one word has been omitted, each blank will have its own set of words to choose from. This is indicated by (i), (ii) and (iii).

Sentence Equivalence

Directions: For each of the following sentences below, select two words from the list which, when inserted into the sentence, are grammatically correct and produce two sentences of similar meaning.

Reading Comprehension

Directions: Each passage in this group is followed by questions based on its content. After reading a passage, choose the best answer to each question. Answer all questions following a passage on the basis of what is stated or implied in that passage.

1. Limited capacity at a local level to train salespeople in building relationships and persuasive techniques could significantly _____ project implementation.

   A. goad

   B. ascribe

   C. stymie

   D. vilify

   E. abjure

2. Nowadays, with very few parents formally teaching their children etiquette, it is feared that this behavioural code is becoming _____.

   A. nugatory

   B. foppish

   C. ineffable

   D. furtive

   E. arcane

3. Opting for a longitudinal study allows for high levels of (i) _____, clarity and validity when assessing developmental changes over time. As the authors note, prior studies have opted for cross-sectional designs which often require more (ii) _____ statistical manipulation in order to achieve comparable samples.

Blank (i)	Blank (ii)
fidelity	opprobrious
diffidence	involute
indolence	invective

4. However, recent data suggests that the majority of the diversity of bird species is due to ecological pressures rather than sexual ones. One of the reasons there may have ever been a debate is that species under sexual selection are often much more (i) _____ and so are studied more commonly than the more (ii) _____ species that make up a much larger proportion on the diversity of the planet.

Blank (i)	Blank (ii)
winsome	Quixotic
wizened	Munificent
ignoble	Lacklustre

5. Whenever the children of the neighbourhood kicked their ball into the old man's garden, he would unleash such a tirade that all the children scarpered immediately. The old man had the well-earned reputation of being the local (i) _____ on account of his (ii) _____. If any parent dared to question him over his behaviour towards the children, the old man would (iii) _____ them for what he termed 'lax parenting'.

Blank (i)	Blank (ii)	Blank (iii)
curmudgeon	insipidness	mollify
astringent	reticence	venerate
iconoclast	irascibility	lambaste

6. It is widely accepted by economists that increasing unemployment rates (i) _____ a (ii) _____ of criminal activity. This well documented relationship (iii) _____ the argument that ensuring jobs and economic opportunities for marginalised and disaffected groups should be a central tenet of policies which seek reduce criminal activity.

Blank (i)	Blank (ii)	Blank (iii)

enumerates	proliferation	dissipates
alleviates	actualisation	bolsters
engenders	dichotomisation	obviates

7. In the face of the realisation of these _____ traits, some individuals freely choose to distract themselves from the engendered anguish they feel and proceed with an inauthentic existence.

   A. equivocal

   B. puerile

   C. innate

   D. obtuse

   E. congenital

   F. luculent

8. Amongst other things, the Cold War was a battle of two nation's egos. Both the US and the Soviet Union were _____ that their philosophy and ideology was superior.

   A. petrified

   B. noisome

   C. provident

   D. obdurate

   E. adamant

   F. suspicious

9. It is thought that more robust professional development, which both supports and helps new teachers to advance subject knowledge and professional skills, is required to improve retention rates. Unfortunately, with ever-tightening school budgets, professional development is often considered to be _____.

   A. dispensable

   B. petulant

   C. spurious

   D. expendable

   E. stentorian

   F. opprobrious

10. Space is also a limiting factor in coral reefs. There are few gaps in the coral and so much of the time species have evolved to be _____ when it comes to occupying space.

    A. foppish

    B. competitive

    C. prosaic

    D. ruthless

    E. meretricious

    F. hermetic

11. There was little direction in the early stages which resulted in several _____ plans. This, unfortunately, meant that the likelihood of success was vanishingly small.

    A. ulterior

    B. caustic

    C. florid

    D. rudimentary

    E. transitory

    F. inchoate

12. Arthur was a true _____: he had attended every railway convention in his state for the past twenty years and showed no sign of stopping any time soon.

    A. nadir

    B. zealot

    C. demagogue

    D. curmudgeon

    E. fanatic

    F. philistine

Questions 13-16 refers to the following passage:

Return the drinking age to 18 and then enforce the law. The current system, which forbids alcohol to Americans under 21, is widely flouted, with disastrous consequences. Teaching people to drink responsibly before they turn 21 would enormously enhance public health. Now, high school and college kids view dangerous binge drinking as a rite of passage. The current law, passed in all 50 states in the 1980s, was intended to diminish the number of

traffic deaths caused by young drunk drivers. It has succeeded in that, but tougher seatbelt and D.U.I. rules have contributed to the decrease, too. Raising the drinking age hasn't reduced drinking, it's merely driven it underground, to the riskiest of settings: unsupervised high school blowouts and fraternity parties that make "Animal House" look quaint. This age segregation leads the drinking away from adults, who could model moderation.

13. This passage is primarily concerned with:

    A. Explaining why underage drinking is dangerous.

    B. Cautioning young people against drinking underage.

    C. Explaining the history of drinking laws in the USA.

    D. Arguing for a reduction of the legal drinking ages in the USA.

    E. Glorifying underage drinking.

14. According to the passage, what is the biggest benefit of lowering the legal drinking age?

    A. Lowering the drinking age would reduce the number of drink driving incidents caused by young people.

    B. Lowering the drinking age would encourage healthier and more responsible drinking behaviours amongst young people.

    C. Lowering the drinking age would increase tax revenues from alcohol.

    D. Lowering the drinking age would irradiate dangerous binge drinking.

    E. Ensure that young people could be supervised while they drink.

15. Select the sentence which clarifies a misconception.

16. The word 'model' in this context most nearly means:

    A. Establish

    B. Condone

    C. Impose

    D. Petrify

    E. Demonstrate

Questions 17-20 refers to the following passage:

What has been said about the formation of ideas and judgments concerning the public apply as well to the distribution of the knowledge which makes it an effective possession of the members of the public. Any separation between the two sides of the problem is artificial. The discussion of propaganda and propagandism

would alone, however, demand a volume, and could be written only by one much more experienced than the present writer. Propaganda can accordingly only be mentioned, with the remark that the present situation is one unprecedented in history. The political forms of democracy and quasi-democratic habits of thought on social matters have compelled a certain amount of public discussion and at least the simulation of general consultation in arriving at political decisions. Representative government must at least seem to be founded on public interests as they are revealed to public belief. The days are past when government can be carried on without any pretence of ascertaining the wishes of the governed. In theory, their assent must be secured. Under the older forms, there was no need to muddy the sources of opinion on political matters. No current of energy flowed from them. Today the judgments popularly formed on political matters are so important, in spite of all factors to the contrary, that there is an enormous premium upon all methods which affect their formation.

17. The main purpose of this passage is:

    A. To condemn autocratic systems of government.

    B. To urge the general public to become more active in politics.

    C. To mandate governments to show strong leadership in times of crisis.

    D. To document the changing relationship between governments and the general public.

    E. To explain the democratic process.

18. The highlighted sentence is an example of the author showing:

    A. Candidness

    B. Determination

    C. Inquisitiveness

    D. Pomposity

    E. Paucity

19. Which statements are correct, according to this passage?

    A. Previously in history, it was not necessary for governments to pay attention to popular public opinion.

    B. Effective propaganda is necessary for a government to be elected.

    C. Governments must at least be seen to be responsive to public opinion in order to be successful governors.

    D. The democratic system is inherently flawed.

    E. The public are generally disinterested in politics.

20. In the context in which it appears, "compelled" most nearly means:

A. Prolonged

B. Obliterated

C. Nullified

D. Necessitated

E. Caused

Section 5: Quantitative Reasoning

Allotted Time: 35 minutes

Number of Questions: 20 questions

1. A bingo machine contains numbers from 1 to 150 inclusive.

Quantity A	Quantity B
The probability of the number being selected containing a 5.	$\dfrac{8}{75}$

A. Quantity A is greater

B. Quantity B is greater

C. The two quantities are equal

D. The relationship cannot be determined from the information given

2. $f(x) = \dfrac{1}{(x - 1)^2}$

Quantity A	Quantity B
f (0.5)	3

A. Quantity A is greater

B. Quantity B is greater

C. The two quantities are equal

D. The relationship cannot be determined from the information given

3. Two work colleagues, Oscar and Isaac decide to drive to the beach after work. Oscar takes a more direct route which allows him to travel at a speed of 50 mph. Isaac takes a more scenic route, but can only travel at 42 mph. Oscar gets to the beach in 30 minutes. Isaac arrives at the beach 20 minutes later.

Quantity A	Quantity B
The additional number of miles Isaac drove compared to Oscar.	8

A. Quantity A is greater

B. Quantity B is greater

C. The two quantities are equal

D. The relationship cannot be determined from the information given

4. Sophie bought her car for $15,000. After the first year, the car was work $12,000 and after the second year it was worth $9000.

Quantity A	Quantity B
The percentage decrease at the end of year 1.	The percentage decrease at the end of year 2.

   A. Quantity A is greater

   B. Quantity B is greater

   C. The two quantities are equal

   D. The relationship cannot be determined from the information given

5. Triangle ACE and triangle BCD are both isosceles. Line BD is parallel with line AE.

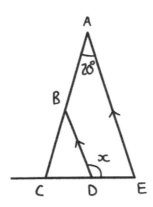

Quantity A	Quantity B
x	110 degrees

   A. Quantity A is greater

   B. Quantity B is greater

   C. The two quantities are equal

   D. The relationship cannot be determined from the information given

6. x + y = 10 and 3x + 4y = 36

Quantity A	Quantity B
x	y

   A. Quantity A is greater

    B. Quantity B is greater

    C. The two quantities are equal

    D. The relationship cannot be determined from the information given

7. $x^2 - 9 = 0$

Quantity A	Quantity B
x	2

    A. Quantity A is greater

    B. Quantity B is greater

    C. The two quantities are equal

    D. The relationship cannot be determined from the information given

8. A cylinder has a height of 4 cm and a radius of 2 cm, as shown.

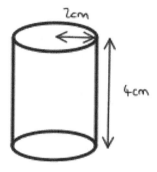

Quantity A	Quantity B
The volume of the cylinder.	The volume of a sphere with radius 2 cm.

    A. Quantity A is greater

    B. Quantity B is greater

    C. The two quantities are equal

    D. The relationship cannot be determined from the information given

9. A square can be drawn to connect the center of four circles (as shown). If the area of each circle is 25π, which expression gives the area shaded green?

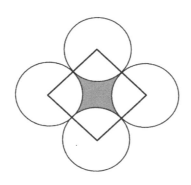

A. 25π

B. $25 - 6.25\pi$

C. $100 - 25\pi$

D. $50 + 25\pi$

E. 100π

10. $9^2 \times 4^x \times 5^2 = 3^2 \times 10^2$. Find x.

A. 1

B. 2

C. 3

D. 4

E. 5

11. $\dfrac{2x - 2y}{y} = \dfrac{51}{17}$. Find $\dfrac{x}{y}$.

A. $\dfrac{5}{2}$

B. $\dfrac{6}{7}$

C. $\dfrac{2}{5}$

D. $\dfrac{3}{4}$

E. $\dfrac{1}{2}$

12. $4.3 \times 10^4 + 2.4 \times 10^4 + 15 \times 10^3$

Which of the following values is equal to the expression above?

    A. 82×10^5

    B. 82×10^4

    C. 8.2×10^2

    D. 8.2×10^3

    E. 82×10^3

13. Use the axes to calculate the area of the shape ABCDE.

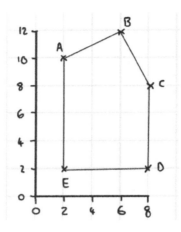

    A. 40

    B. 44

    C. 48

    D. 52

    E. 56

14. An artist is trying to decide which of his paintings he should show in his upcoming exhibit. The exhibit space can only fit 5 of his paintings in. If the artist has 7 paintings in total, how many different combinations of painints are possible?

    A. 10

    B. 15

    C. 21

    D. 28

    E. 30

15. ABDE is a rectangle. The length of side BD is 70. If the length of BC is four sevenths the length of BD, and the length of AB is three sevenths the length of BD, what is the length of AC?

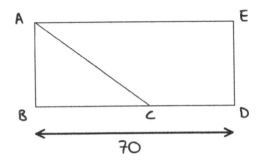

A. 20

B. 30

C. 40

D. 50

E. 60

16. Dora ask her friend to pick a number between 1 and 9. Dora multiplied this number by 3, added 6, multipled by 2, added 1 and, finally, divided by 5. Dora ended up with 11. What was the original number selected by Dora's friend?

A. 2

B. 7

C. 8

D. 4

E. 9

17. Find the point at which the lines y = -x + 2 and y = -2x + 6 intersect.

A. (0,0)

B. (1,2)

C. (3,0)

D. (4,2)

E. (4,-2)

The graph shows the number of male and female students who achieved each grade in a mathematics exam. And refers to questions 18-20:

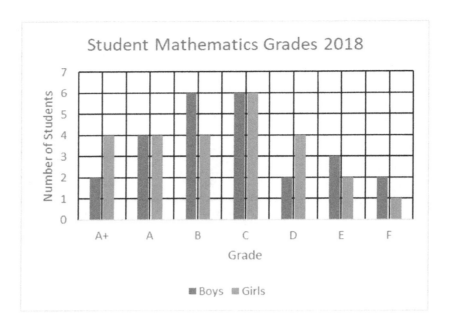

18. For which grade was the ratio of boys to girls the lowest?

    A. A+

    B. A

    C. B

    D. D

    E. E

19. What percentage of boys achieved a D or above?

    A. 40%

    B. 52%

    C. 60%

    D. 75%

    E. 80%

20. What percentage of girls achieved a D or below?

    A. 5%

    B. 14%

    C. 28%

    D. 30%

    E. 35%

Section 6: Verbal Reasoning

Allotted Time: 30 minutes

Number of Questions: 20 questions

Text Completion

Directions: Each of the passages below has had one, two or three words omitted. For each of the blacks, select a word that best fits the meaning of the sentence and passage. If more than one word has been omitted, each blank will have its own set of words to choose from. This is indicated by (i), (ii) and (iii).

Sentence Equivalence

Directions: For each of the following sentences below, select two words from the list which, when inserted into the sentence, are grammatically correct and produce two sentences of similar meaning.

Reading Comprehension

Directions: Each passage in this group is followed by questions based on its content. After reading a passage, choose the best answer to each question. Answer all questions following a passage on the basis of what is stated or implied in that passage.

1. Many teachers will testify that students often disregard the methods they are taught and opt for their own _____ versions, which often yield inaccurate or unsatisfactory results.

   A. synoptic

   B. ersatz

   C. polemic

   D. turgid

   E. vociferous

2. The pressure on real estate agents to sell houses quickly leads to high levels of _____ throughout the selling process.

   A. chicanery

   B. detraction

   C. vestige

   D. abasement

   E. indolence

3. Some scholars suggest that, historically, differences in education levels of males and females was (i) _____ of the gender pay gap. This is supported by the fact that the gender pay gap has narrowed substantially in the second half of the twentieth century as women have (ii) _____ more education and training. While it is clear that raising female human capital through education has partly closed the gender pay gap, there are a number of other factors at play which also contribute to earning disparities.

Blank (i)	Blank (ii)
antecedent	wrangled
parsimonious	shunned
officious	accumulated

4. In order to (i) _____ the most effective policies and invest in the most appropriate inputs, studies need to be conducted on individual developing nations and (ii) _____ solutions developed based on the countries available resources and expertise.

Blank (i)	Blank (ii)
ascertain	ebullient
quell	commodious
stipulate	bespoke

5. Perhaps, the greatest attribute that a politician should possess is (i) _____. Given the volume of questions they face daily, it is unlikely that they will be able to meet every single question with a concise and (ii) _____ response. Given this, being able to talk on a topic generally, while constructing more targeted responses in one's head, is a (iii) _____ skill.

Blank (i)	Blank (ii)	Blank (iii)
loquaciousness	insolent	obsolete
perpetuity	cogent	cardinal
indigence	vivacious	monolithic

6. The prosecuting barrister (i) _____ the notion that a crime this barbaric merited a severe punishment. The barrister's opening gambit presented the defended as a (ii) _____, sadistic and all-round dangerous individual who deserved to experience the full weight of the law for their (iii) _____.

Blank (i)	Blank (ii)	Blank (iii)

precluded	profuse	transgressions
mollified	capricious	sophism
reaffirmed	erudite	derision

7. When evaluating the success of a project, an overreliance on participant interviews is _____. Interviews are inherently subjective by nature, and therefore, they are subject to bias (both intentional and unintentional).

   A. edacious

   B. vitriolic

   C. inadvisable

   D. furtive

   E. sedulous

   F. injudicious

8. He managed to save up enough money to buy his house outright after years of being _____.

   A. parsimonious

   B. polemic

   C. frugal

   D. inept

   E. incredulous

   F. shrill

Questions 9-12 refers to the following passage:

America has endured more than one mass shooting per day so far this year, according to the Gun Violence Archive, a non-profit research organisation. This weekend, the country suffered two more. The carnage started on the morning of August 3rd, when a man armed with an AK-47 killed 20 people in El Paso, Texas. Hours later, a man outfitted with body armour, an assault rifle and a handgun killed 10 people in Dayton, Ohio. After such events Democrats often call for stronger gun-control laws; Republicans recommend reforming the country's mental-health system or banning violent video games. Finding common ground has proved almost impossible. Polls suggest that Americans tend to favour the Democrats' approach. According to a survey conducted in March 2019 by the Associated Press-NORC Center for Public Affairs Research (AP-NORC), 67% of Americans support stronger gun laws, up from 55% in October 2013; 10% think they should be relaxed (down from about 14%); 22%

think the existing gun laws should be left alone (down from 28%). Roughly 60% of Americans think military-style semi-automatic weapons, of the sort used in this weekend's shootings, should be banned outright.

9. The main purpose of the passage is to:

   A. Call for an outright ban on military-style semi-automatic weapons.

   B. Illustrate how contentious the issue of gun control is in the USA.

   C. Report the consequences of lax gun control laws.

   D. Refute arguments supporting stricter gun control laws.

   E. Explain why many Americans are in favour of tighter gun control laws.

10. Select all that apply. The examples highlighted are included in order to:

    A. Ground the authors argument in current events.

    B. Impress upon the reader the severity of the situation regarding fun control.

    C. Explain the Republican position on gun control.

    D. Provide context to the current debate on gun control.

    E. Illustrate that shootings in the USA are isolated events.

11. Select the sentence which details two contrasting positions.

12. Select the reason why the author has chosen to include the highlighted phrase.

    A. To add credibility to a statistic.

    B. To praise those who conducted the research.

    C. To convince the reader that stricter gun laws are needed.

    D. To refute questionable statistics.

    E. To avoid ambiguity.

Questions 13-16 refers to the following passage:

In the Spring of 2016, a 12-year-old named Andrew Bellow spent three and a half months in a psychiatric hospital in Chicago. His hair, which he liked to wear cropped, grew long and unkempt. He forgot what it felt like to wear shoes because he was allowed to wear only hospital socks. He missed months of school and couldn't go outside. He celebrated his 13th birthday at the hospital, where he said the walls were bare and there was little to do. Doctors had agreed Bellow was ready to be discharged about six weeks after he arrived, but the Illinois Department of Children and Family Services, which is his legal guardian, couldn't find anywhere for him to go. Bellow is one of hundreds of children in the care of DCFS who are held each year inside psychiatric hospitals for

weeks or months, even though they have been cleared to leave. Instead of moving on to a foster home or residential treatment centre - a less restrictive facility where children attend school and lead more normal lives - these children have languished in secure mental health facilities, the consequence of the child welfare agency's failure to find them appropriate placements. These unnecessary hospitalizations are another failure for a state system that has frequently fallen short in its charge to care for Illinois' most vulnerable children, who suffer from conditions such as severe depression or bipolar disorder.

13. The passage is primarily concerned with:

    A. Calling for an increase in funding for psychiatric services in Chicago.

    B. Condemning the actions of the doctors in the psychiatric hospital.

    C. Exposing the failures of Illinois Department of Children and Family Services.

    D. Appealing for a home for Andrew Bellow.

    E. Explaining the psychological needs of children in care.

14. The author includes the brief segment about Andrew Bellow in order to:

    A. Appeal for the reader to help this individual.

    B. Garner sympathy from the reader.

    C. Expose the scandal of Bellow's treatment.

    D. Explain how children end up in psychiatric hospitals.

    E. Vividly describe Bellow's appearance.

15. What would the author consider to be the most appropriate solution to the problem presented in the passage?

    A. An improvement in the living conditions in psychiatric hospitals for children.

    B. Relaxing of the rules in psychiatric hospitals for children.

    C. Systemic reform in the Department of Children and Health Services.

    D. Increasing efforts to diagnose mental health conditions in young people.

    E. Providing more mental health support services to children in foster homes.

16. In this context, the word languished, most nearly means:

    A. Defected

    B. Vindicated

C. Liberated

D. Malingered

E. Mouldered

Questions 17-20 refers to the following passage:

In the aftermath of Hurricane Katrina in August 2005, while stranded New Orleanians flagged down helicopters from rooftops and hospitals desperately triaged patients, crude oil silently gushed from damaged drilling rigs and storage tanks. Given the human misery set into motion by Katrina, the harm these spills caused to the environment drew little attention. But it was substantial. Nine days after the storm, oil could still be seen leaking from toppled storage tanks, broken pipelines and sunken boats between New Orleans and the Mississippi River's mouth. And then Hurricane Rita hit. Oil let loose by Katrina was pushed farther inland by Rita three weeks later, and debris from the first storm caused damage to oil tankers rocked by the second. All told, the federal agency overseeing oil and gas operations in the Gulf of Mexico reported that more than 400 pipelines and 100 drilling platforms were damaged. The U.S. Coast Guard, the first responder for oil spills, received 540 separate reports of spills into Louisiana waters. Officials estimated that, taken together, those leaks released the same amount of oil that the highly publicized 1989 Exxon Valdez disaster spilled into Alaska's Prince William Sound — about 10.8 million gallons.

17. What is the main purpose of this passage?

    A. To prompt the US government to help communities effected by hurricanes.

    B. To articulate the magnitude of the problem of oil spills after hurricanes.

    C. To impress upon the reader how catastrophic Hurricane Katrina and Hurricane Rita were.

    D. To encourage environmental agencies to assist in cleaning up oil spills.

    E. To condemn the inaction of the U.S. Coast Guard.

18. What purpose does the highlighted sentence serve in this passage?

    A. The highlighted sentence is included to expose the inaction of the US Coastguard.

    B. The highlighted sentence encourages the reader to sympathise with communities affected by hurricanes.

    C. The highlighted sentence refutes the idea that hurricanes cause oil spills.

    D. The highlighted sentence summarises the authors position.

    E. The highlighted sentence asks the reader to consider why these oil spills didn't get as much attention as other, similarly sized spills.

19. What reason does the author give for the oil spills being ignored in the wake of Hurricane Katrina.

A. The media failed to publicise the spills.

B. Emergency services were preoccupied by saving lives and helping communities directly impacted by the hurricane.

C. Environmental issues are not high enough on the government agenda.

D. The oil companies downplayed the severity of the leaks.

E. The US. Coastguard did not deem the oil leaks to be a pressing concern.

20. Select the sentence which quantifies the magnitude of the oil spills.

Answers

Section 1: Issue Topic

Compare your response to the advice in the analytical writing area to calculate your score.

Section 2: Argument Topic

Compare your response to the advice in the analytical writing area to calculate your score.

Section 3: Quantitative Reasoning

1. A
2. C
3. D
4. B
5. D
6. B
7. D
8. C
9. D
10. B
11. A
12. E
13. B and C
14. E
15. D
16. A and B
17. D
18. B
19. C
20. D

Section 4: Verbal Reasoning

1. (C) stymie
2. (E) arcane
3. (i) fidelity (ii) involute
4. (i) winsome (ii) lacklustre
5. (i) curmudgeon (ii) irascibility (iii) lambaste
6. (i) engenders (ii) proliferation (iii) bolsters
7. (C) innate (E) congenital
8. (D) obdurate (E) adamant
9. (A) dispensable (D) expendable
10. (B) competitive (D) ruthless
11. (D) rudimentary (F) inchoate
12. (B) zealot (E) fanatic
13. D
14. B
15. "It has succeeded in that, but tougher seatbelt and D.U.I. rules have contributed to the decrease, too."
16. E
17. D
18. A
19. A and C
20. E

Section 5: Quantitative Reasoning

1. A
2. A
3. A
4. B
5. B

6. B

7. D

8. A

9. C

10. A

11. A

12. E

13. D

14. C

15. D

16. B

17. E

18. B

19. E

20. C

Section 6: Verbal Reasoning

1. (B) ersatz

2. (A) chicanery

3. (i) antecedent (ii) accumulated

4. (i) ascertain (ii) bespoke

5. (i) loquaciousness (ii) cogent (iii) cardinal

6. (i) reaffirmed (ii) capricious (iii) transgressions

7. (C) inadvisable (F) injudicious

8. (A) parsimonious (C) frugal

9. B

10. A, B and D

11. "After such events Democrats often call for stronger gun-control laws; Republicans recommend reforming the country's mental-health system or banning violent video games."

12. A

13. C

14. B

15. C

16. E

17. B

18. D

19. B

20. "All told, the federal agency overseeing oil and gas operations in the Gulf of Mexico reported that more than 400 pipelines and 100 drilling platforms were damaged."

Score Conversion

Your final GRE® report will contain 3 scores that combine for your total score. One for each of Analytical writing, Verbal and Quantitative. Your Writing will be scored from 0 to 6 increasing by half point increments. Both of the other sections are scored 130 -170, increasing by one point increments. It is however, not white as simple as it seems.

For the multiple choice sections, you will score one point for every question that you get correct. So, you must answer them all. So, for example if you get 38 questions correct in quantities reasoning, then your raw score will be 38 for quantitative reasoning. That's all fine and easy so far; however, you won't ever see those scores as they are converted into scaled scores before you see them. The reason for this is to keep it all fair year on year and to account for the fact that the test may be slightly easier some years compared to others. In conversion from Raw to scaled scores, two things happen: Adaptive testing and Equating.

Adaptive Testing

Most of the people who take the GRE® will be on a computer, and this means that you will; have an adaptive test. All this means is that how well you do on the first section (of each type) will affect the difficulty of the questions that you get in the second sections (of that type). For example, if you do really well in the first of the Verbal Reasoning tests, then the next test that you will get for verbal reasoning will have harder questions.

This means that you could end up with harder questions than somebody else, and therefore getting less total questions correct. This is the point of adaptive testing however and a complex system allows for the variation in questions and will make sure that you get a fair score. It is a very good system that allows a big differentiation for those taking the test. It's not worth trying to figure out which question bank you have received, just focus on getting as many questions correct as you can.

Equating

Equating is another system used by the ETS to allow tests to be compared to each other. If you sat one exam early in the year and then a friend sat the exam later in the year but it was easier, you would feel upset if they got the same number of questions correct and their score was the same as yours. This is exactly what equating fixes. Again it's a complex system that you don't really need to understand, but essentially it means that your score will compare the standard of your test as well as your performance on it, so that you can be compared to people who sat the GRE® early in the year, late in the year and also from different years.

Analytical Writing Scoring

For Analytical writing each of the argument and issue essays are graded separately from 0-6, in 0.5 [point increments]. It is done by a trained grader working for ETS but then also by a computer algorithm which is designed to look for writing skills. If the compute and human are within one point of each other, you get the

average of the two. If they are further than this apart, a second trained ETS human grader will mark the essays and the average of the two human scores is used.

Then, your final score is an average of the two essay task scores that you have been given. Below is the scoring rubric for the essays:

Issue Grading Text

Score 6 - Outstanding

In addressing the specific task directions, a 6 response presents a cogent, well-articulated analysis of the issue and conveys meaning skillfully.

A typical response in this category:

- Articulates a clear and insightful position on the issue in accordance with the assigned task.

- Develops the position fully with compelling reasons and/or persuasive examples.

- Sustains a well-focused, well-organized analysis, connecting ideas logically.

- Conveys ideas fluently and precisely, using effective vocabulary and sentence variety.

- Demonstrates superior facility with the conventions of standard written english (i.e., grammar, usage and mechanics), but may have minor errors.

Score 5 - Strong

In addressing the specific task directions, a 5 response presents a generally thoughtful, well-developed analysis of the issue and conveys meaning clearly.

A typical response in this category:

- Presents a clear and well-considered position on the issue in accordance with the assigned task.

- Develops the position with logically sound reasons and/or well-chosen examples.

- Is focused and generally well organized, connecting ideas appropriately.

- Conveys ideas clearly and well, using appropriate vocabulary and sentence variety.

- Demonstrates facility with the conventions of standard written english, but may have minor errors.

Score 4 - Adequate

In addressing the specific task directions, a 4 response presents a competent analysis of the issue and conveys meaning with acceptable clarity.

A typical response in this category:

- Presents a clear position on the issue in accordance with the assigned task.

- Develops the position with relevant reasons and/or examples.

- Is adequately focused and organized.

- Demonstrates sufficient control of language to express ideas with acceptable clarity.

- Generally demonstrates control of the conventions of standard written english, but may have some errors.

Score 3 - Limited

A 3 response demonstrates some competence in addressing the specific task directions, in analyzing the issue and in conveying meaning, but is obviously flawed.

A typical response in this category exhibits **one or more** of the following characteristics:

- Is vague or limited in addressing the specific task directions and in presenting or developing a position on the issue or both.

- Is weak in the use of relevant reasons or examples or relies largely on unsupported claims.

- Is limited in focus and/or organization.

- Has problems in language and sentence structure that result in a lack of clarity.

- Contains occasional major errors or frequent minor errors in grammar, usage or mechanics that can interfere with meaning.

Score 2 - Seriously Flawed

A 2 response largely disregards the specific task directions and/or demonstrates serious weaknesses in analytical writing.

A typical response in this category exhibits **one or more** of the following characteristics:

- Is unclear or seriously limited in addressing the specific task directions and in presenting or developing a position on the issue or both.

- Provides few, if any, relevant reasons or examples in support of its claims.

- Is poorly focused and/or poorly organized.

- Has serious problems in language and sentence structure that frequently interfere with meaning.

- Contains serious errors in grammar, usage or mechanics that frequently obscure meaning.

Score 1 - Fundamentally Deficient

A 1 response demonstrates fundamental deficiencies in analytical writing.

A typical response in this category exhibits **one or more** of the following characteristics:

- Provides little or no evidence of understanding the issue.

- Provides little or no evidence of the ability to develop an organized response (e.g., is disorganized and/or extremely brief).

- Has severe problems in language and sentence structure that persistently interfere with meaning.

- Contains pervasive errors in grammar, usage or mechanics that result in incoherence.

Score 0

- Off topic (i.e., provides no evidence of an attempt to address the assigned topic), is in a foreign language, merely copies the topic, consists of only keystroke characters or is illegible or nonverbal.

Score NS

- The essay response is blank.

A good essay therefore should...

- Make sense logically.

- Be precise in its discussion of the issue and the author's stance on the issue.

- Include support for the author's position that persuades the reader to the author's point of view.

- Be organized and flow smoothly from idea to idea.

- Be well-written with clarity and variation in sentence structure.

Argument Grading Text

Score of 6 - Outstanding

A 6 paper presents a cogent, well-articulated critique of the argument and conveys meaning skillfully.

A typical paper in this category:

- Clearly identifies important features of the argument and analyzes them insightfully.

- Develops ideas cogently, organizes them logically and connects them with clear transitions.

- Effectively supports the main points of the critique.

- Demonstrates control of language, including appropriate word choice and sentence variety.

- Demonstrates facility with the conventions (i.e., grammar, usage and mechanics) of standard written english but may have minor errors.

Score of 5 - Strong

A 5 paper presents a generally thoughtful, well-developed critique of the argument and conveys meaning clearly.

A typical paper in this category:

- Clearly identifies important features of the argument and analyzes them in a generally perceptive way.

- Develops ideas clearly, organizes them logically and connects them with appropriate transitions.

- Sensibly supports the main points of the critique.

- Demonstrates control of language, including appropriate word choice and sentence variety.

- Demonstrates facility with the conventions of standard written english, but may have minor errors.

Score of 4 - Adequate

A 4 paper presents a competent critique of the argument and conveys meaning adequately.

A typical paper in this category:

- Identifies and analyzes important features of the argument.

- Develops and organizes ideas satisfactorily, but may not connect them with transitions.

- Supports the main points of the critique.

- Demonstrates sufficient control of language to express ideas with reasonable clarity.

- Generally demonstrates control of the conventions of standard written English, but may have some errors.

Score of 3 - Limited

A 3 paper demonstrates some competence in its critique of the argument and in conveying meaning, but is obviously flawed.

A typical paper in this category exhibits **one or more** of the following characteristics:

- Does not identify or analyze most of the important features of the argument, although some analysis of the argument is present.

- Mainly analyzes tangential or irrelevant matters, or reasons poorly.

- Is limited in the logical development and organization of ideas.

- Offers support of little relevance and value for points of the critique.

- Lacks clarity in expressing ideas.

- Contains occasional major errors or frequent minor errors in grammar, usage or mechanics that can interfere with meaning.

Score of 2 - Seriously Flawed

A 2 paper demonstrates serious weaknesses in analytical writing.

A typical paper in this category exhibits **one or more** of the following characteristics:

- Does not present a critique based on logical analysis, but may instead present the writer's own views on the subject.

- Does not develop ideas or is disorganized and illogical.

- Provides little if any relevant or reasonable support.

- Has serious problems in the use of language and in sentence structure that frequently interfere with meaning.

- Contains serious errors in grammar, usage or mechanics that frequently obscure meaning.

Score of 1 - Fundamentally Deficient

A 1 paper demonstrates fundamental deficiencies in analytical writing.

A typical paper in this category exhibits **one or more** of the following characteristics:

- Provides little or no evidence of the ability to understand and analyze the argument.

- Provides little or no evidence of the ability to develop an organized response.

- Has severe problems in language and sentence structure that persistently interfere with meaning.

- Contains pervasive errors in grammar, usage or mechanics that result in incoherence.

Score of 0

A typical paper in this category is:

- Off topic (i.e., provides no evidence of an attempt to respond to the assigned topic), is in a foreign language, merely copies the topic, consists of only keystroke characters, or is illegible or nonverbal.

Score of NS

- Blank.

A good essay therefore...

- Develop its ideas logically.

- Limit its discussion to identifying and explaining the parts of the argument that are relevant to the essay task.

- Be organized and connect ideas smoothly.

- Include support for the main points of the author's analysis.

- Be well written.

The Final Day and Night, Last Advice

It's the night before the big exam. The hard work is done, your preparation has come to an end, and now is the ideal time to calm down your nerves and make sure that you're ready to enter the exam hall well rested and confident in your ability to write an outstanding exam essay.

So that's it, you've followed the hints and tips, you've worked through the questions and you're prepared and ready to go. So, what to do now? Cram? Panic? No! It's not all over, preparation for the final exam itself is crucial. So please make sure you follow the tips below to garauntee that you get the final 10% of your preparation correct, it really is that crucial.

Rule 1. Be Safe.

Don't change something at the last minute, you wouldn't want to make any last minute changes or start experimenting with different things at this stage. Trust that you are suitably prepared. Don't try new memorization techniques, new diets, and medications sleep routines on the last day. The time for trying new things has passed. Stick to what you know and trust!

Rule 2. Proper Preparation prevents poor performance.

Steve Jobs used to only have a very specific wardrobe so that he didn't have to think about what to wear in the morning; he allowed himself more mental capacity for the tasks at hand as a result. We're not suggesting that you go quite that far, but it may be worthwhile to pack your bag the day before the exam. Lay out your clothes, check that you have everything. This way, when you wake up in the morning you can prepare safe in the knowledge that all you need to do is to get yourself to the test and put into practice everything that you have learned.

Rule 3. Get your sleep.

As it is incredibly important throughout your time studying, there is no surprise that the night before the exam you try and get a good night's rest. Don't stay up late cramming; it won't help, believe us. Do: relax, wind down, and do something enjoyable. Set an alarm so you don't panic. This is really crucial that you try and get a good rest before his day of the examination.

Rule 4. Have a good diet.

This is another rule that applies as much to daily life as it does to the night before the exam, however it is crucial. Eat well the day before, drink plenty of water, eat fruit and vegetables. Don't have loads of carb heavy foods which will make you feel groggy and tired the next day. All the small things will have a big impact in the end.

Rule 5. Glance through your notes.

If you have completed your exercises, practice tests and prepared properly, you will have heaps of notes. Read them on the final day. Remember mistakes that you have learned from.

Don't go over new challenging concepts but make sure that you reflect on things you have learned and are comfortable with. The idea is to refresh and to allow yourself to be confident the day before, so avoid too much of a challenge, just keep the information fresh.

Rule 6. Meet your study group the day before.

If you've had group together studying, you will want to talk about the test. But tomorrow (test day) is not the day to do this, you want to be making sure that you can squash all nerves the day before and on the day you don't want other people's nervous energy ruining your confidence.

Make sure your friends know that you will want to focus and meet them for a coffee the day before instead. Get all the nervous chatter out of the way and end the conversations with a confident topic. It is really important that you are in a good headspace the day of the test.

Rule 7. Turn it off.

That's right. The S-word. Social Media. We strongly advise that on the night before the exam you turn off your devices. Unless there is something crucial that you need, watching a YouTube video of a cat sneaking up on people is not good preparation, and you may well end up tiring yourself out and getting worked up.

Go for a walk instead, and you can get straight back on the Social Media after the exam and realize you haven't missed much!

Rule 8. Get rid of other distractions too.

It's not just devices and Social Media that can distract. It may be a partner, housemate or family member. It could be you record collection. On the night before, you want utmost calm and peace, so if that means that you need to politely tell your housemate that you don't want them playing music's at 0100 in advance, then so be it!

If you follow this advice, complete the exercises in this book, you will do well!

Go to the exam room prepared, concentrated and relaxed. Good luck, you got this!

Signing Off

So that's it, you've worked hard and completed the exercises and the tests. Rest assured that you've done all you can to prepare, and let us take this opportunity to wish you the very best of luck in your GRE®. As always, please stay in touch and send your results/success stories to info@innotion.org.

Made in the USA
Las Vegas, NV
15 January 2021